SLOW KNOWLEDGE AND THE UNHURRIED CHILD

This book explores the relationship with time in early childhood by arguing for the valuing of slow pedagogies and slow knowledge. Alison Clark points to alternative practices in Early Childhood Education and Care that enable a different pace and rhythm, against the backdrop of the acceleration in early childhood and the proliferation of testing and measurement. Diverse approaches are explored to enable an 'unhurried child' and less hurried adults.

Slow Knowledge and the Unhurried Child is divided in three parts. Part 1, Reasons to be slow, looks at the pressures in Early Childhood Education and Care to speed up and for children to be 'readied' for the next stage. The book then explores different relationships with time for young children and educators. Part 2, Slow pedagogies and practices, explore some of the forms slow practices can take including outdoors, in the studio, in everyday routines, through stories, in pedagogical documentation and in 'slow' research. Part 3, Moving forward, shows what a 'timefull' approach to ECEC can look like, whilst debating the challenges and possibilities that exist.

The book serves as a catalyst for urgent discussion about the need to slow down in early childhood education and teacher education and explores case studies of where slow practices in early childhood education are already happening. It will be a key reading for researchers, practitioners and policy-makers about the relationship with time in early childhood and the importance of taking a longer view.

Alison Clark is Professor of Early Childhood Education at the University of South-Eastern Norway and Honorary Senior Research Fellow at the Institute of Education, University College London, UK.

Contesting Early Childhood

Series Editors: Liselott Mariett Olsson and Michel Vandenbroeck

This ground-breaking series questions the current dominant discourses surrounding early childhood and offers instead alternative narratives of an area that is now made up of a multitude of perspectives and debates.

The series examines the possibilities and risks arising from the accelerated development of early childhood services and policies, and illustrates how it has become increasingly steeped in regulation and control. Insightfully, this collection of books shows how early childhood services can in fact contribute to ethical and democratic practices. The authors explore new ideas taken from alternative working practices in both the western and developing world, and from other academic disciplines such as developmental psychology. Current theories and best practice are placed in relation to the major processes of political, social, economic, cultural and technological change occurring in the world today.

Rethinking Environmental Education in a Climate Change Era
Weather Learning in Early Childhood
Tonya Rooney and Mindy Blaise

Slow Knowledge and the Unhurried Child
Time for Slow Pedagogies in Early Childhood Education
Alison Clark

The Decommodification of Early Childhood Education and Care
Resisting Neoliberalism
Michel Vandenbroeck, Joanne Lehrer and Linda Mitchell

For more information about this series, please visit: www.routledge.com/Contesting-Early-Childhood/book-series/SE0623

SLOW KNOWLEDGE AND THE UNHURRIED CHILD

Time for Slow Pedagogies in Early Childhood Education

Alison Clark

Routledge
Taylor & Francis Group

LONDON AND NEW YORK

Cover image: © Getty Images

First published 2023
by Routledge
4 Park Square, Milton Park, Abingdon, Oxon OX14 4RN

and by Routledge
605 Third Avenue, New York, NY 10158

Routledge is an imprint of the Taylor & Francis Group, an informa business

British Library Cataloguing-in-Publication Data
A catalogue record for this book is available from the British Library

ISBN: 9780367508807 (hbk)
ISBN: 9780367508814 (pbk)
ISBN: 9781003051626 (ebk)

DOI: 10.4324/9781003051626

Typeset in Bembo
by Apex CoVantage, LLC

For Product Safety Concerns and Information please contact our EU representative:
GPSR@taylorandfrancis.com
Taylor & Francis Verlag GmbH, Kaufingerstraße 24, 80331 München, Germany

CONTENTS

FOREWORD

A study by Brecht Peleman et al. (2020) showed that three-year-olds in Kindergarten in Flanders spend up to 20 to 30% of their time waiting. The reason is that their teachers want to hurry because of the pressure they experience to teach these children what is expected from them in the next year by the next teacher. As a result, much of their time and of the children's time is spent on organising the transition times to lunch, to outdoors, or to other activities as "efficiently" as possible, and the group must wait until the last child is ready. In order not to waste any time, children are kept silent during the waiting time. It is but one of the abundant examples we find in early childhood in many countries of what I have named in previous publications (Vandenbroeck 2017) as 'the Olympic games of development', a vision on child development as sports discipline, aligned with the Olympic slogan 'citius, altius, fortius' (faster, higher, stronger). It is what Alison Clark labels as "accelerated childhoods". In this book she critically looks at the increasing impatience of the educational system. Her critical analysis offers a broad view on how early childhood education is related not only to the entire 'hurrying' educational system from preschool to higher education, but also to the broader society. She holds out a mirror to us, reflecting on the fundamental question of 'what is education for?' And in doing so, she also questions what educational research is for, as she relates the hurrying early childhood also to a hurrying science.

What this book uniquely offers the reader is not only fine analysis and reflection on the times we are living in. Alison Clark urges us to stop for a moment and look at what we are doing in early childhood education. A particularly important contribution of this book is that it presents to us the possibility of not taking the highway, as she describes several possibilities of sideways. She rightly argues that these sideways are not the same as taking a step back, that slowing down is not just a romantic idea of going back to an unproductive era or a longing for a past that never existed. On the contrary, it is about taking time to think about what matters, about gaining depth, about preparing for unpredictability, about expecting the unexpected. The fastest way from A to B may very well be a straight line, but that may not necessarily be the line that prepares one for real life or for the life that we wish to be real.

Alison Clark explores what slow pedagogy is all about. Therefore, she offers choices, alternative pathways and these are both theoretically deepened and illustrated with many observations of children's experiences and interactions. The ways in which these cases are presented relates theory with fine analyses of daily practice and strong ethical concerns.

What is true for the hurried child is equally true for the hurried scientist. Increasingly, we find alerts on social media from researchers who are stepping out of the academic rat race where the publication pressure leads to 'slicing' findings into ever smaller publishable parts, data fixing, plagiarism, and other forms of scientific fraud, leading to ever higher numbers of article retractions. Science risks to be reduced to what is publishable as relevance tends to be reduced to the impact factor of the journal where the results are published. Innovation and reflection are to be concealed in 6,000 words, an abstract and a bibliography. The work of Alison Clark is a strong antidote to this illness in the educational research community. It is an exercise in listening, acknowledging that listening and giving voice (for example, to children) does take time and cannot or should not be formatted in a 6,000-word limit and an impact factor.

With this book, Alison Clark does exactly what the book series 'Contesting Early Childhood' aims at: offering alternatives and, in her words, time to rethink. The book should be recommended reading not only for future early childhood scholars, but also for practitioners and policy-makers. I sincerely wish they will take the time to read and think. As the Belgian-French singer songwriter Jacques Brel sang, there are two kinds of time: the time that waits and the time that hopes. The present book offers us time that hopes.

Michel Vandenbroeck

Peleman, B., Van Avermaet, P., and Vandenbroeck, M., 2020. Early learning opportunities for children at risk of social exclusion. Opening the black box of preschool practice. *European Early Childhood Education Research Journal*, 28, 21–42.

Vandenbroeck, M., 2017. Introduction: Constructions of truth in early childhood education. *In:* M. Vandenbroeck, ed. *Constructions of neuroscience in early childhood education.* London: Routledge, 1–19.

PREFACE

Time and context

Books hold time in a particular way – the time in which the book is conceived and written and subsequently published and read and perhaps even returned to.

The evidence of the wider context is inevitably going to be apparent in a book that takes *time* as a central theme; in this case in relationship to early childhood education, pedagogy and practices and the wider higher education environment.

My ideas have grown over the past ten years or more. The research study that forms the central frame started in January 2020. It seems important to state this starting point as three months into the study we were facing a global pandemic. This seismic medical, social, economic and political crisis placed *time* centre stage. A changed relationship with the clock and the passage of time was not a uniform experience. Some people experienced the necessity to speed up in order to meet the urgent demands of the moment. Rapid decision-making was needed to source more medical equipment and to organise learning online. For many others time slowed, including those needing to protect their health. Time and its impact on us became hard to ignore.

Tipping point

The pandemic has created a 'stutter in the narrative' (Rose 1999) about every institution, raising questions about what it means to be a school, a university, an office, a shopping centre, church or mosque, particularly for those periods when many people were unable to gather. This has offered the possibility for rethinking essential purposes and how these link to values. This stutter, a break in a confident narrative, has resonance for education and early childhood education. This period of uncertainty may provide the opportunity to reassess what are the core purposes of ECEC and to what extent long established values are represented in current practice. It is perhaps a tipping point. This book, I hope, may contribute to such a reassessment and provide questions and examples about what and how things could change. It is part of a series on Contesting Early Childhood that sets out to challenge dominant discourses in the field of early childhood education. This book does not promote one particular theoretical frame but looks at what theoretical and methodological approaches have been used and continue to emerge for slow pedagogies. The aim is to present complex ideas clearly in order to suggest creative alternatives that draw widely on international examples from within and beyond early childhood practice. The intention is not to present a naïve call to 'turn the clock back' to an ideal past but to promote discussion among the early childhood community about what different relationships with time in ECEC can look like and why such reflection is necessary.

Alison Clark
Orkney, Scotland
April 2022

ACKNOWLEDGEMENTS

Many conversations have underpinned this book. My ideas have been deeply influenced by the children I have met through my earlier studies involving listening to young children, by the insights they have given and questions they have provoked about time, play, belonging and place. I am very grateful to everyone who has taken part in this research and in the discussions that came before and after. My special thanks to those interviewed (see Appendix) for their generous engagement with this theme and for being part of this collaborative thinking. Likewise, my thanks to Emma Clarkson, Karina Girvan, Donna Green, Grace Haines, Lorna Hill, Katie McCracken, Melanie O-Leary, Annette Ledger and Liz Turbitt for taking part in the focus group to discuss initial findings and to everyone who took part in the virtual reading group.

My thanks to my colleagues and to students at the University of South-Eastern Norway with whom this book has grown and taken shape

The generosity of The Froebel Trust has provided the opportunity to pursue this topic in depth. Their support has extended to hosting events and recording seminars. This has been invaluable in enabling wider access to the debate and to enable others to contribute their wisdom and creativity including Jo Albin-Clark, Sharon Colilles, Chris Pascal and Gemma Paterson who were speakers at the Urgency of Slow seminar to mark the end of the study.

My thanks to John Horton and Tracy Hayes for their workshop that reminded me writing is allowed to sometimes be enjoyable and to Agnes Bosanquet whose academic blog: 'Slow academic' accompanied me along the way.

I have benefitted from the generosity of my critical readers Karyn Callaghan and Margaret Carr and especially to Peter Moss for ongoing discussions and interest. Any errors of fact or judgement are mine alone.

My continued thanks to Jonathan who has lived with this book during lockdown and to the wonderful Ren for their timely support.

PART 1

Reasons to be slow

Part 1 makes the case for the reasons to be slow in early childhood. This will look firstly at the pressures on ECEC to speed up, for children to be 'readied' for the next stage and to go for easily transmitted and captured 'fast knowledge' before exploring ways to think about slow knowledge in relation to young children.

Different approaches to time are introduced starting with 'clock time' and notions of 'wasted time' as applied to early childhood. This is followed by a discussion of the distinctive emphasis on 'play time' by investigating temporal dimensions to thinking about play including a historical perspective focusing on Froebelian approaches. This leads to alternative constructs for relating to time that can be applied to early childhood education including 'timefullness' (Swinton 2016); 'expansive time' (Povey et al. 2021); 'stretched time' (Cuffaro 1995) and 'whiling time' or 'worthwhile time' (Jardine 2008, 2012, 2013). Part 1 ends by building on these constructs to articulate definitions of slow pedagogies and slow knowledge.

DOI: 10.4324/9781003051626-1

1
ACCELERATED CHILDHOOD

Introduction

This book grows out of an increasing concern about acceleration in education and in early childhood in particular. The need to 'run ever faster to maintain our place in the world' as expressed by the German sociologist Hartmut Rosa (2019: 415) is being felt across all sectors of education including Higher Education. I set out in these opening chapters to point to some of the signs of this acceleration before turning to alternative narratives that seek to reconsider the relationship with time, pace and rhythm in early childhood education.

I begin with taking Rosa as my guide and his observations about escalation and acceleration. Rosa in his book *Resonance* (2019) makes the case that modernity is based on a relationship to the world that has escalation at its core and links the compulsion to escalate with the drive to compete. He comments:

> I am concerned with the relationship to the world of a sociocultural forma-
> tion that is capable of stabilizing itself only dynamically, i.e., that is dependent
> on systematic escalation in the dimension of economic growth, acceleration,
> and rates of innovation in order to reproduce its structure and maintain its
> formative status quo.
>
> *(Rosa 2019: 406)*

His critique of contemporary society has strong parallels with what has been happening in education and in early childhood education (ECEC). He continues:

> regardless of how successfully we live, work, and busy ourselves this year,
> individually and collectively, next year we will have to be a little faster, more
> efficient, more innovative, better, if we want to maintain our place in the

DOI: 10.4324/9781003051626-2

world – and the year after that the bar will be set a little bit higher. In fact, success, strength and efficiency in the present are directly proportional to the strength of the compulsion to escalate in the future.

(Rosa 2019: 407)

The phrase 'bar set a little bit higher' – alerts us to the connection between speed and expected performance. We always have more to prove, more to measure, higher to jump.

Living in the shallows

Stephen Ball's critique of neoliberal education over several decades has drawn attention to the increasing need for children and educators to 'jump higher'.

> In regimes of performativity, experience is nothing, productivity is every-thing. Last year's efforts are a benchmark for this year's improvement – better exam and test results, more students going into higher education, more pub-lications, more research grants. We must keep up; strive to achieve the new and ever more diverse targets which we set for ourselves in appraisal meet-ings; confess and confront our weaknesses; undertake appropriate and value-enhancing professional development; and take up opportunities for making ourselves more productive, ensuring what O'Flynn and Petersen (2007: 469) call a 'targeted self' or what Gee (1999: 46) refers to as the 'shape-shifting portfolio person.'

(Ball 2016: 1054)

Performativity here is closely linked to productivity and measurable outcomes. Measurement can be seen to be the dominant discourse in neoliberalism that has had a profound impact on early childhood education and care (ECEC) (Moss 2019; Clark 2020; Brogaard Clausen et al. 2015; Robert-Holmes and Bradbury 2016; Vandenbrœck 2020; Robert-Holmes and Moss 2021). There is a temporal dimen-sion to an emphasis on the easy to measure, as I have discussed in a chapter in *Transforming Early Childhood in England* (Cameron and Moss 2020) that paved the way for this research:

> Filling out a predefined checklist or baseline about what a child can do at any one moment in time can be far quicker to achieve than carrying out an in-depth observation or sitting and talking together. 'Saving time' can be an important factor in a professional culture where measurement dominates, especially when practitioners find themselves needing to collect a greater volume of standardised information about children, and at more frequent intervals. In a measurement culture what is measured matters (Volante 2018) and acquires increasing visibility.

(Clark 2020: 137)

Gert Biesta draws attention to the link between the desire for acceleration within educational systems, the prevalence of performativity and the notion of impatience:

> I am inclined to argue that what we find here is predominantly an impatient look. Not only do we find a desire to put as much world as possible into the child or student. We also find a desire to do this as quickly and cheaply as possible, to constantly monitor and measure the effectiveness and efficiency of the operation, to make teachers' salaries dependent on the extent to which they succeed in producing pre-specified 'learning outcomes.'
>
> *(Biesta 2012: 99)*

This describes the overarching need to 'get there faster' which at the same time opens up the question of where is the destination; what is the purpose of education? Biesta takes up this challenge and argues persuasively for what he describes as the 'beautiful risk of education' (2013) that acknowledges the 'fundamental complexity and openness of all educational processes and practices' (2012: 99).

> All this suggests that the education of the will is a question of patience and perseverance, a process that needs time and attention. There is, in other words, no quick fix where it concerns the encounter with resistance and the ability to be 'in dialogue' with the world, with what is other and different.
>
> *(Biesta 2012: 98)*

Having time to be in dialogue 'with what is other and different' alerts us to the important dimensions to education that can be absent if the dominant regimes lead to us only skimming the surface of learning and relationships. Ball refers to this as depthlessness: 'The neo-liberal subject is malleable rather than committed, flexible rather than principled – essentially depthless' (Ball 2010: 126). Robert-Holmes and Moss (2021: 90–117) consider the consequences of 'neoliberal imagery' on how young children, parents and early childhood centres are viewed:

> The image of the 'poor' child, a reproducer of knowledge, values and identity, and yet to be realised human capital; the image of the parent as consumer and realised human capital seeking to achieve and maintain the best returns on the capital; the image of the early childhood centre as business and as factory or processing plant, a site for investing in the efficient achievement of certain outcomes, the first stage in the development of human capital and readying the child for the next stage, compulsory primary schooling.
>
> *(2021: 106)*

The roles of early childhood 'workers' or educators if viewed in this way become 'competent technicians' (Osgood 2009) or 'economic custodians' (Robert-Holmes and Moss 2021: 109).

Hurried Higher Education

I have become aware of the increasingly hurried nature of Higher Education, as an academic who has worked in the sector in the UK and more recently in Norway. This wider educational frame, beset with tightly packed curricula and performance indicators, is relevant for a study that sets out to explore the possibilities and challenges in re-examining the relationship with time in early childhood education and with early childhood education students. The underlying values, structures and procedures in the Higher Education sector will in turn impact on the preparation of early childhood educators and on day-to-day engagement with young children.

Time pressures in HE can have an emotional toll on those who need to work within and manage the systems. I have experienced undertaking marking of scripts, for example, under a 'traffic light' system designed to monitor efficiency. The late return of marked scripts was given a red light to indicate failure to make the tight deadline. This system seemed to induce fear rather than encourage improvements in the quality of feedback. It is an example of needing 'to run ever faster', as Rosa commented.

Doreen Massey, writing in 2002, addressed the issues of time in relation to academic life in an editorial entitled 'Time to think':

> to have the time and may be the confidence to worry away at something. To read things, the works of others, not simply to find out what they say but as moments in a longer, slower process of musing something over. To *re*-read things. To go back to old material maybe to rework it.
>
> *(Massey: 259)*

Massey conveys the need to think in depth and to have the capacity and perhaps, as she says, 'confidence' to keep burrowing away at an idea without a prescribed outcome or output in mind: 'It is a kind of richness and depth of intellectual texture.' She links this deep thinking to the wider frame in which learning is taking place beyond freeing an isolated portion of time in a diary, to what is of worth: "The issue of having time to think is more than one of whether we can preserve a free afternoon here and there. It is more about the overall pace and atmosphere of things; it is about what is valued" (Massey: 259).

This is directly relevant to thinking about re-examining the relationship with time in early childhood education. There are underlying issues at stake about the pace and atmosphere and what is of value. One of the triggers for this need for attention to pace in higher education is what Massey describes as 'the tyranny of the immediate'– short-term deadlines, activities, responses, constantly intrude upon the possibility of getting down to something bigger, longer-term, more strategic. Writing in 2002, she refers to dealing with the flood of emails. This has continued but there is now an added layer of immediacy of engagement required as part of academic life with social media platforms. As Twitter declares: 'Twitter is what's happening and what people are talking about right now' (Twitter 2006).

Within this 'real time' very fast flowing stream it is easy for yesterday to disappear. It holds time in a particular way and impacts on our use of time. Facebook adds a further dimension to its relationship with present and past by sending subscribers 'memories' as this platform calls specific posts chosen by the algorithm from previous years and launches them back into present timelines.

Massey points out that depth of thinking might occur slowly but it is the attention to pace that is important and the culture within which the intellectual work occurs. Without it she argues intellectual life is in danger of becoming 'thinner' (p. 261). The concept of 'thinness' connects with Ball's observation of neoliberal education living in the shallows. Ideas around what shape professional and pedagogical depth can take will be returned to throughout this book.

Slow scholarship

There is a growing movement within Higher Education to challenge acceleration (for example, O'Neill 2014; Bosanquet et al. 2020; Harrison-Greaves 2016; Lasczik Cutcher and Irwin 2017; Collett et al. 2018). Mountz et al. (2015) make the case for slow scholarship together with a feminist ethics of care to challenge the neoliberal university: 'Good scholarship requires time: time to think, write, read, research, analyze, edit, and collaborate. High quality instruction and service also require time: time to engage, innovate, experiment, organize, evaluate, and inspire' (p. 1237).

Canadian academics Barbara Seeber and Maggie Berg develop the case for slow scholarship further in *The Slow Professor: challenging the culture of speed in the academy* (2016). Seeber and Berg echo several of Massey's observations and call for finding ways for 'timelessness' or timeless time. This sense of being absorbed in the present moment Seeber and Berg link to Csikszentmihalyi's concept of flow (1990, 1997). I will return to an exploration of this state of flow when exploring slow practices in different environments (Chapter 5) and with materials (Chapter 6) in the studio. Slow scholarship is part of the Slow Movement that I turn to next.

Attention to slow

The Slow Movement has been one response to accelerated living, beginning with the Slow Food movement, begun by the culinary writer Carlo Petrini as a challenge to fast food and multinational corporations (Tishman 2018: 4). Honoré's popular book 'In Praise of Slow' (2004) documented the spread of ideas about alternatives to fast-paced living across different areas of everyday life including food, medicine, cities and education. Honoré's experience of time-pressed parenting was one of the catalysts for writing the book, faced with the appeal of the 'one-minute bedtime story':

> At the time, I am locked in a nightly tug-of-war with my two-year-old son, who favours long stories read at a gentle, meandering pace. Every evening,

> though I steer him towards the shortest books and read them quickly. We often quarrel. 'You're going too fast,' he cries. Or, as I head for the door, 'I want another story!' . . . Taking a long, languid stroll through the world of Dr Seuss is not an option. It is too slow.
>
> *(Honoré 2004: 2)*

In this example the power of the clock is evident and the impact of the need to accelerate on everyday routines between young children and their parents.

Honoré emphasises that the Slow Movement strives for balance rather than perpetual slow motion:

> The Slow Movement is not about doing everything at a snail's pace. Nor is it a Luddite attempt to drag the whole planet back to a pre-industrial utopia . . . the Slow philosophy can be summed up in a single word: balance. be fast when it makes sense to be fast and be slow when slowness is called for. Seek to live at what musicians call the *tempo giusto* – the right speed.
>
> *(Honoré 2004: 13)*

This opens up interesting questions for thinking about Early Childhood Education: what might 'balance' look like between fast and slow and what is the 'right speed'? The chapters that follow seek to explore these questions.

The Hurried Child

I first heard the phrase 'The hurried child' in conversation with a Japanese colleague, Mari Mori, just before the pandemic. Debates about 'hurriedness' and childhood are not a 21st century phenomena. *The Hurried Child: growing up too fast, too soon* was the title of a book written by the American psychologist David Elkind, first published in 1981, making the case for the pressure on children from parents, school and the media. I found reference in an online medical dictionary to 'Hurried child syndrome', described as 'a condition in which parents overschedule their children's lives, pushing them hard for academic success'. Maurice Holt draws parallels between the inherent problems with fast food and 'fast schooling'. He describes a fast school model as follows:

> The engagement between teacher and learner should be as predictable as possible, and variation between one teacher and another can be offset by scripting the learning encounter and tightening the form of assessment. If the purpose of schooling is to deliver the knowledge and skills that business needs, this approach cuts costs, standardizes resources, and reduces teacher training to a school-based process. Above all, the efficacy of the operation can be measured and the results used to control it and its functionaries – the teachers. But if schools exist to equip students with the capacity to address

the unpredictable problems of adulthood and to establish themselves in a world of growing complexity, then crucial disadvantages emerge.

(Holt 2002: 268)

The relevance of equipping learners to face unpredictability and complexity may be one of the lessons the education sector chooses to take from the pandemic.

Pandemic-temporal narratives

Young children's experiences of the pandemic have been diverse and deeply affected by their social and economic circumstances and national context (Pascal and Bertram 2021). In the early days of the first 'lockdown' in the UK in March 2020, I observed a rush to set up arrangements for 'home school', driven by the challenge of how to manage working from home and looking after young children. Many schools and organisations posted online materials for parents to use with their children. Some were play-based, others provided more formal worksheets. The rules about what school and early childhood education looked like needed to be rethought, with little warning. Teachers' and parents' roles also changed with both perhaps dealing with heightened anxiety and the need to be seen as productive. Performativity and the need to be seen as 'busy' took on a new dimension. Amongst these rapid changes were calls to hold on to the value of play. A headline in the Guardian newspaper on 21 April 2020 read: 'Don't turn your home into a school' (Ferguson 2020) quoting the University of Cambridge academic, Professor Paul Ramchandani.

The discourse about the relationship to time and learning became louder in the UK as a possible end to the pandemic was thought to be in sight in Spring 2021. The rhetoric of 'catching up' emphasises the language of competition, of education as running a race. Children need to catch up with their lost learning in order to meet the benchmarks set. Catchup is a visible and powerful indicator of the push towards accelerated childhoods. A bulletin from the Institute of Fiscal Studies, (Sibieta 2021), much quoted in the media at the time, is a clear indicator that this is primarily an economic concern rather than pedagogical or social – warning how many thousands of pounds individuals (and the exchequer) are set to lose in lost earnings over a lifetime. Here children are viewed as human capital or future human capital within a neoliberal worldview. And the solutions proposed favour increasing learning time:

Increasing learning time

We therefore need to think of big and radical ways to increase learning time. This could be extending the school year, lengthening the school day, mass repetition of whole school years or summer schools. And there is sound evidence that increasing instructional time can yield positive effects. Given we're trying to compensate for half a year of lost normal schooling, such measures would likely be necessary for a few years. I am not in a position to advocate for any of these options. Indeed, schools and teachers will probably have a much better idea of what is possible with the right resources. But everything should be on the table and we should be engaged in a national debate about the merits and feasibility of all of them.

(Sibieta, L. (2021)
The crisis in lost learning calls for a massive national policy response.
Observation 15291. Institute for Fiscal Studies.)

The desire for increasing learning time expressed in this bulletin views education simply through an economic lens (Robert-Holmes and Moss 2021: 93). This represents a transmissive pedagogy (Oliveira-Formosinho and de Sousa 2019) and a view of a child as an empty vessel to be filled – as quickly as possible. There has been a ground swell of opposition to these ideas from some parents and educators, highlighting the need for the social above economic 'drivers', a recovery curriculum linked to the importance of time to play.

This is the context in which my research on 'Slow knowledge and the unhurried child' has taken place. Reflecting on Rosa's comments earlier, my research considers:

> *'Are we asking young children and those who work with young children to run ever faster to maintain their place and ours in the world?*
> *What alternatives are there rooted in different early childhood practices and traditions that can be reclaimed?'*

The study

The study, based on a purposive sample, focuses on key informant interviews with twenty early childhood and primary researchers, educators and advisors across eleven countries: England, Scotland, Wales, Norway, Japan, Denmark, Portugal, Israel, USA, Canada and Australia (see Appendix). The participants were chosen for their engagement in research and practice with young children up to eight years of age that relate in various ways to what might be defined as slow pedagogies and slow knowledge, both terms of which will be explored in detail in the subsequent chapters. The study, funded by the Froebel Trust, explores perspectives on the contemporary context of early childhood education and the range of pressures that may be experienced by adults and children within the system. The study looks intentionally at where 'slow practices' are happening now and in the past. By exploring different types of slow practice, the hope is to demonstrate one of a number of alternative narratives to the dominant measurement culture. Examples will be included of how engaging at a different pace and rhythm can be experienced by Early Childhood Education students. Questions will be raised about who might slow practices benefit most and what might be of lasting value for young children and adults? The initial findings have been discussed in a focus group with nine early childhood educators and students from England and Scotland, engaged in a range of provision including private and public sector and in diverse roles including an early years pedagogue, Forest school practitioner, arts educator and a nursery manager.

*

The book is divided into three sections. Part 1 makes the case for the reasons to be slow in early childhood. Chapter 2: Clock time, examines different approaches to time in education and in early childhood education including how notions of business and 'wasted time' may relate to the concept of performativity referred to in this introduction. This is followed in Chapter 3 by a focus on play and the relationship with time, opening up different ways of conceptualising time. This chapter includes attention to the application of Froebel's ideas about play. Part 1 ends with Chapter 4 by exploring definitions of slow pedagogies and slow knowledge. Three interconnected themes that emerged from these discussions are discussed: 'Being with', 'Going off track' and 'Diving deep.'

Part 2 provides critical reflection on what attention to time can look like in ECEC. This section expands on 'What are the slow practices and in what contexts are they happening?'

Chapter 5 looks at 'Slow practices in place'. Examples move from outdoor environments, through in-between spaces to classroom interiors and the relationship between design, pedagogy and time. Chapter 6 looks in more detail at the range of slow practices that can emerge working with young children and materials, including in the dedicated environment of the studio. Chapter 7 explores how pedagogical documentation can be understood through a temporal lens (Carr and Lee 2019). The focus moves to everyday routines in Chapter 8, looking specifically at the relationship between slow practices and mealtimes as a starting point for change. This chapter also raises questions about how slow pedagogies view children's past and future as well as valuing the present moment. Chapter 9 seeks to explore the question: 'how can you be slow with a book?' in contrast to the concept of the 'one-minute bedtime story' discussed earlier (Honoré 2004). Different timescales are investigated to see what is gained from young children 'living with' a story over many months and in having time to develop and act out their own stories. Chapter 10 looks critically at how slow pedagogies connect with listening to young children in research and practice. This includes examples of visual and multimodal methodologies including the Mosaic approach (Clark 2017, 2020) and video reflection.

Part 3, the final Chapter 11, makes the case for an expansive view of time in ECEC and examines what a 'slow and patient' kindergarten might look like including the challenges and possibilities that might result.

Conclusion

Thinking about time in relation to early childhood education is a complex but important task. The historians Cathy Burke and Ian Grosvenor draw on the work of Michel Serres to emphasise this complexity:

> Time is a multi-faceted concept. It can be viewed as historical, scientific or mathematical. It can be imagined, experienced and measured. It can be

theorised as geographically rigid, with constant measurable distances or as percolated:

> Time does not always flow according to a line . . . but rather, according to an extraordinarily complex mixture, as though it reflected stopping points, ruptures, deep wells, chimneys of thunderous acceleration, rendings, gaps – all sown at random, at least in a visible order.
>
> *(Serres 1990: 59 in Burke and Grosvenor 2003: 121)*

Each chapter ends with a series of questions intended as a catalyst for further discussions to connect with your own experiences and contexts.

Questions

1   In what ways have you observed changes in the relationship between time and education in recent years?
2   What do you see as the main factors that may contribute to young children experiencing ECEC as hurried?
3   What might 'balance' look like in terms of the relationship with time in early childhood education?

2

CLOCK TIME

Introduction

Sonnyboy was one of the four-year-olds who took part in Jacqui Cousins's study of 'young talkers and thinkers' as they started school in England (Cousins 1999). This book was one of the first texts I read as I began researching with Peter Moss about listening to young children in the same year that Jacqui's book 'Listening to four-year-olds' was published. Sonnyboy's voice and opinions have remained with me ever since. It is Sonnyboy's observation that 'Time is as long as it takes' that I have kept returning to. Jacqui describes in detail his Traveller background and rich story telling. She noticed, in particular, how Sonnyboy didn't like to be rushed:

> Sonnyboy was obviously unrushed at home. His family was not ruled by the clock and there was a different rhythm to their lives. Most significantly, I found that any attempt to hurry Sonnyboy or to impose school routines which did not allow him to go into depth with what he was doing or to complete activities to his satisfaction was met with frustration and irritation. This was most notable when 'bells and breaks' interrupted his enjoyment of those activities which required prolonged exploration or needed sustained concentration and perseverance on his part.
>
> *(Cousins 1999: 14)*

This chapter discusses the impact of the clock on everyday practices in ECEC. I will centre this exploration around comments from participants in my research interviews and focus group who are researching and teaching in different ECEC and primary school contexts. Building on concepts introduced in Chapter 1, I will look at accounts of busyness, hurry and 'wasted time'. This discussion is set against

DOI: 10.4324/9781003051626-3

the background of the implications of education policies in different national contexts on how time and temporality are materialised.

Pacini-Ketchabaw explores the idea of 'clock time' in ECEC by looking at the temporal dimensions to everyday life in early childhood settings through the relationships between animate and inanimate things – considering the clock as a producer and enabler or excluder of practices:

> The clock structures both the arrangement of children and educators in the classroom and the very practice deployed throughout a regular day. At the same time, it produces particular knowledges about what it means to be an educator and what it means to be a child in an early childhood classroom. The clock is fundamental to how early childhood education is understood, organized, and enacted.
>
> *(Pacini-Ketchabaw 2012: 155)*

This demonstrates the importance of thinking about the temporal dimension to teaching and learning by arguing how we think about time impacts on how we see children and childhood and about what it means to be an educator. This points to the link between thinking about time and reflecting on the purposes of education – it leads us into fundamental questions, as I began to explore in Chapter 1. Reassessing the relationship with time takes us from the macro to the micro, as Pacini-Ketchabaw points out, from questions about purpose to how each day is structured and what practices are encouraged or forbidden. Drawing on examples from Sonnyboy again, down to the micro level of whether he was stopped midway through telling a story, or absorbed in exploring worms in the garden or making large constructions with his friends (Cousins 1999: 14).

Curricula frameworks hold time in particular ways and sometimes have unintended consequences. I have been reflecting back on one of my first teaching roles in the 1980s as a Reception class[1] teacher with children who were four and five years of age. I had recently been on Highscope training day and was interested in introducing a way of working that I hoped would give more agency to the children, based on the principle of 'Plan, Do and Review' (Hohmann et al. 1979). I rearranged my timetable to give periods in the week when different groups of children could work through a range of activities at their own pace. I have been thinking about how the organisation might have impacted on the children. My reflection almost thirty years later would be, 'How much freedom did the children in my class have to plan their own learning? What impact did my interpretation of this curriculum have on children's relationship with the clock?' The intervening decades in the UK have seen a plethora of curriculum changes that have introduced a range of different time practices to primary and early childhood education. The introduction of the National Curriculum in the late 1980s followed by the National Literacy Strategy (NLS) (1998) brought significant changes to the structure of the school day. The introduction of the 'Literacy Hour' is perhaps the most explicit example of the impact on the relationship with time where the graphics chosen to illustrate the approach depicts a clock-face, clearly set out to show how each minute of the hour should be spent (Jewitt and Jones 2005). The Literacy hour for children in Key Stage One and Two[2] was divided into two periods of 15 minutes for whole class teaching, followed by 20 minutes for group and independent work and a final ten minutes for a whole class 'reviewing, reflecting and consolidating teaching points and presenting work covered'.

Clock time, busyness and a 'waste of time'

I began by discussing with my research participants what they felt were the main pressures on early childhood education at present. Setting to one side the immediate difficulties of working with young children through a pandemic our discussions looked at the underlying pressures and tensions on educators and on children and on policies that may be contributing to such pressures.

Emma Dyer (see Appendix) reflected on her experiences starting as a Reading Recovery teacher[3] in an English Primary school in 2010:

> So, I suppose, there's this pressure in schools to perform and to be able to do certain things at certain times, hit certain milestones at certain points, but then not necessarily developmental milestones, much more milestones in terms of what they can achieve or what they can demonstrate. So, children are supposed to be reading fluently by the age of six, and writing and because the curriculum is so heavily reading and writing led in England. It filters back and back and back further and further back. So that idea of exploring slowly and doing a range of different things. I'm not saying it's gone, but then that pressure starts earlier and earlier.
>
> It's like a sort of funnel that funnels up to Year One [five- to six-year-olds] at which point you have to demonstrate that you can read proficiently . . . . the curriculum in terms of the reading and writing curriculum, you have to be able to write in certain styles, you have to be able to write a report and you have to be able to present things in different ways. Children really need a lot of tuition if they're going to do that. And so it has to start early. And if they don't, then the school will . . . be punished essentially or will 'fail' in some way.
>
> *(Emma Dyer, interview, June 2020)*

Emma drew attention to the downward pressure on the younger children in primary school to meet the literacy targets: 'It filters back and back'. I shall return to this phrase shortly. This links to Stephen Ball's comments earlier about performativity. The downward pressure to reach prescribed benchmarks can squeeze out other practices that cannot be easily measured. Emma continues:

> So when I joined my school in 2010, and every afternoon Reception and Year One would have 'Busy time'. And it was a chance for . . . everything

was just put out all across all the tables, play things and Lego and books and all those sort of things and they were given an hour or so to just choose where they wanted to play and what they wanted to do. And then by 2012 that was just gone . . . because it was seen as 'a waste of time'.

It was interesting the word 'busy' anyway. I mean, the irony was that it was felt that the children weren't busy enough . . . they had to be more busy doing something more structured really.

(Emma Dyer)

What is valued as a worthwhile use of time? Emma's example here illustrates how what is viewed as of importance can change from a daily occurrence to becoming labelled as a waste and removed from the timetable. As Emma reflects it is ironic that this period for freeplay was referred to as 'busy time', but it had become seen as unproductive – a waste, not producing the learning goods. Within this relationship with the clock there is an erosion of young children's opportunities to play. It has become a casualty of the need to be seen to perform. This opens up a discussion about play and time that will be explored in more detail in Chapter 3.

Hurried educators

Emma's account was one of many participants who discussed experiences of hurry as educators or observing hurried children, and hurried learning, as I discussed in Chapter 1.

I also think learning is being hurried. So there's this expectation that children will do certain things at a certain time. And I would argue that children need this time and space to pursue their own interests. I think tick box assessments which everybody has been encouraged to use limits children's capacity to comprehend the full systems of their knowledge. And again . . . some knowledge is valued over others, and it results in children being left behind . . . And this is a big one I think for practitioners so practitioners that want to fight the systems, they're up against the regulators expectations of them. And there's a fear of reprisals.

(Lynn McNair, interview, September 2020)

Lynn McNair, Head of an under fives centre and Lecturer in Early Childhood practice and Froebel in Scotland, indicates here the link between the expectations of progress measured by limited tick box assessment can intensify the sense of hurry on educators. She raises the question of the energy needed to challenge the existing status quo in early education and the possible concern of negative repercussions. This gives a sense of regulatory regimes creating a surveillance culture. This governance may exist in several forms: external regulatory bodies beyond individual ECEC institutions but also from within institutions, from parents and also self-governance.

Lorna Hill, a member of my focus group commented:

> I work with two-year-olds, and I find that sometimes I like to sit back for quite a while and just watch [the children] and their play and I often feel like I am being pressured by other staff to do something. So I'm sitting and observing. I'm listening. I'm watching their actions, I'm thinking this is what I need to be doing and I feel as though some staff are trying to rush onto the next task: 'What are you going to put out today? whereas I would rather a child have time and time again to revisit so they become confident, and then they develop their own explanations, so that you can then plan something that would be meaningful to them.
>
> *(Lorna Hill, focus group, April 2021)*

It is as if Lorna needs to 'steal back time' in order to sit with the children and to respond to their actions.

Parents' expectations may add to the sense of urgency, as Júlia Oliveira-Formosinho commented, from her perspective as an early childhood teacher educator and researcher in Portugal:

> I've seen the acceleration of the life of children in preschools to increase with the awareness of society and of parents about the importance of the early years, the importance of preschool. So then, the, pressures for schoolification instead of looking at preschool as an avenue, a pathway to help children to research the world, to research with their 'one hundred languages'. Normally the tendency is to answer through schoolification.
>
> *(Júlia Oliveira-Formosinho, interview, October 2020)*

Júlia draws attention to the pressures on preschools for 'schoolification' (for example, Bradbury 2019) where the prime focus is on preparing young children for the next stage of their education in school. This is in contrast to approaching ECEC as distinct in its own right providing opportunities for children to 'research the world, to research with their hundred languages', drawing on Malaguzzi's phrase about the multiple ways children can express themselves (Edwards et al. 2012; Cagliari et al. 2016). We will discuss the downward pressure in education in the following section.

Expectations from the media may add a further dimension to how time is managed for young children, as Elkind highlighted (1981). Pressures from the media was a specific factor identified by Mari Mori, an early childhood teacher educator in Japan:

> In Japan, especially entering into elementary school [pressure] is the biggest issue not just for families but also for the pressure on preschool and

kindergarten day nursery teachers, it's a really the big concern of most parents and in mass media as well.

Mari Mori identified the last month in preschool before children joined elementary school as particularly intense and scripted for young children and their educators:

> The school year starts in April and finishes in March. So in the month of March, especially for the teachers of the five-year-olds' classroom it has a negative [effect], feel the pressure is on. The children have to sit for 45 minutes and learn how to hold the pencils and 'can you jump in' and 'can you skip?', for example.
>
> *(Mari Mori, interview, September 2020)*

Here Mari highlights the issue of the transition to school as a particularly time-pressured period for both educators and children. The future intrudes on the present in a sometimes-forceful way. I will return to this foreshadowing in the next section.

There may also be internal pressures. In reality there may be less of a requirement to hurry than is felt by educators and the pressure to accelerate learning has become internalised: a 'governing of the self' (Foucault 1993; Rose 1999). This can be understood as another indication of the impact of neoliberal performativity as Ball describes:

> Performativity 'works' most powerfully when it is inside our heads and our souls; that is, when we monitor and manage ourselves, when we take responsibility for working harder, faster and better, thus 'improving' our 'output', as part of our sense of personal worth and in the ways we judge the worth of others.
>
> *(2010: 125)*

Kari Carlsen, a Norwegian early childhood teacher educator observed:

> I think many, many, many [educators] are working in a very good way, of course. But I think many of them feel and say that they have no time. So the question of time, they are more or less in a hurry. Maybe they think that they have more constraints than they have? They think that they have more narrow frames than the Framework plan gives the institutions of preschool. I say well, you can do as you like, you have a freedom, but you don't use. I think that they really have a freedom in the Norwegian preschool. They have a freedom that many do not take and take as their own way to shape the everyday life. Because that has something to do with the customs and the traditions and the culture of preschool. And of course, we find that different preschools have rather different cultures . . .. So I think this is about 'feeling' you have permission. This is about freedom and that they do not exercise

this freedom to take the initiative themselves. I think the frames are seen to be more narrow than they really are.

(Kari Carlsen, interview, September 2020)

So Kari's reflection raises the question of how educators can feel there is no time even when working within a curriculum framework such as in Norway that is not tightly scripted. Professional confidence appears to be a key factor here in ceasing the opportunities to exercise freedom and to engage at a different pace.

Differences between the type of provision and work culture in learning environments can impact on how the relationship with the clock is experienced. In this next example, Donna Green, an early childhood pedagogue based in Scotland, reflects on her experiences across her career in a range of different provision:

> But when I look back I started off in what we call a Day nursery and at the time it wasn't driven through checklists so we didn't have teacher inputs and even when we did get teacher input, it still wasn't driven in that way. It was really from the child and I would say probably thinking back, a slow ethic was there then. And really the children led the day . . . It was at an all-year-round facility and then I moved to early years provision that was only operated during school terms, not during the school holidays. At the time I noticed straight away, the pace increased because it was a two-and-a-half-hour session. So there was an expectation there, but there was still an element of really good practice, and at times there was the free flow . . . and then I changed to a school, a big, busy, really affluent area school and the increase in pace increased again. My role was a senior early years officer. The parents had high expectations what they wanted for their children.
>
> *(Donna Green, focus group, April 2021)*

Donna's reflection demonstrates the time constraints part-time sessions can place on young children and educators, especially where the policy demand for more content is squeezed into short periods of time. Annette Ledger explained further about her experience managing a nursery:

> the fact that in nursery, 26 children in in the morning for three hours, then we'd have like literally an hour and then another 26 different children in for another three hours. And the way that works is not conducive to having any time, and as a practitioner, I think there's an element as well of exhaustion because, you give your all as you do we all care so deeply we want to do the right thing and be professional, but when you are so constrained for time and you're thinking on your feet all the time. You're not getting that proper time because then you're tired and you're setting up for next children that coming in and I think there's a real barrier there . . . That's a major challenge.
>
> *(Annette Ledger, focus group, April 2021)*

Timetables and downward pressure

Timetables are one powerful representation of our relationship with time. Jewitt and Jones (2005) investigated how time and space in a classroom in an Inner London Secondary school had been impacted by government educational reforms and teacher interpretations of these changes. They refer to 'policy time' as 'the ways in which time-use is imagined and promoted by policy-makers' and 'time practices' as the teacher responses, to both national policies but also the local context (2005: 206). This is one example of the time practices of an English subject teaching department.

> Time for discussion was rigorously controlled by the teacher, and time pressures were always evident . . . In relation to the vastness of tasks involved, they knew that time was in short supply. It had to be measured, rationed, synchronised, constantly monitored and accounted for; there was no other way of getting the students through the examination. The examination itself – a year or so away was constantly drawn to the attention of students, through spoken reminders, through handouts and through wall displays. In this sense we can speak of a *proleptic* organisation of time: the tasks of the lessons were described to students as anticipations of examination requirements; the final goal had a constant presence in the moment -to-moment activity of the lesson.
>
> *(Jewitt and Jones: 209)*

Jewitt and Jones found how this interpretation of how to prepare students for the GCSE English examination, which for this class was still over a year in the future, contrasted to another school in their study with a very different relationship with time:

> The timings of lessons – their beginnings and ends – were conditional upon the levels of consent offered by the students. Within quite broad limits, students could choose on what activities their lesson time could be spent; teachers' work involved, to an important extent, an intervention in students' activity, which took as its starting point the tempo of learning established by the student.
>
> *(Jewitt and Jones: 207)*

Reflecting on Jewitt and Jones' account, it is not only the policy and curriculum framework but how this is interpreted and enacted in the classroom that appears to be significant here. A proleptic organisation of time can be seen to be one in which future goals 'foreshadow' the 'moment to moment' activities. The 'here and now' had been invaded by the demands of the future. This relates to Emma Dyer's comments earlier about how pressure 'filters back and back' to younger and younger children. This has strong parallels with those models of contemporary

ECEC where assessment and future assessment increasingly cast a long shadow over the present moment.

This is how one of my participants, William Clark, a Key Stage One teacher in an English primary school explained these pressures:

> I think you have to talk to an extent about Key Stage One to get a full understanding of the pressures on early years, having spent time in both year groups, so I am speaking from experience of three years of teaching in Year One, then I moved to Reception (Foundation Stage) and taught for three years then and now I've just started in Year Two, so I'm back in Key Stage One again.
>
> And a lot of the pressures in terms of speed and coverage, and content are ones which come from a place of knowing what is going to be required at a later stage in education. So, knowing that they have to be ready for the phonics screening in Year One means that that pressure gets put into Reception to get them ready for that eventuality, and knowing other pressures which are going to come in Year Two means that the pressures go to Year One where you may say they have to be ready for the kind of challenges that they're going to have in SATs. And then that, again, [the pressure] moves down [the age groups] because you don't have time in the year group itself to get them prepared for that task in its totality it has to be the years below that start that work.
>
> *(William Clark, interview, October 2020)*

It seems clear from William's observations that this can be seen as a 'proleptic' organisation of time, as Jewitt and Jones (2005) describe. The value of the present moment for children becomes almost invisible in the face of what looms ahead. This resonates with Mari Mori's comments earlier about the particular pressure on children and educators in the month before moving from pre-school to school within the Japanese education system. Preparations for and transitions into school routines can bring the relationship with time into sharp relief. Donna Green explained how planning and timetabling impacted on the day-to-day experiences of the children in her role as Senior Early Years Officer in a primary school, working with four-year-olds on starting school:

> So I went on a really big journey there. And when I first started it was very much driven, by the academic and the emphasis on achieving and it took me a long long time to really try to stand my ground in relation to what children need. It was all about planning and timetabling and when you could go to the Gym Hall and who had to go. Children were being timetabled. I had to then do a yearly overview. Its putting children in boxes. I don't know I've not met the children!
>
> *(Donna Green, focus group, April 2021)*

One important aspect of time pressure that underpins many of the discussions in this book is the question of ratios between children and educators. Kate Cowan discussed the impact of such pressures:

> There's a feeling that there's a timetable that we've got to stick to and, and we've got to do it that same way, or else you know something terrible will happen. And I think I definitely thought when I was teaching that there were loads of really interesting moments of learning that I would really love to have kind of zoomed in on and just focused on, but actually you know there were 19 other children and I needed to have eyes everywhere and I needed to be thinking about the bigger picture.
>
> *(Kate Cowan, interview, July 2020)*

The final section in this chapter returns to thinking about young children's sense of working with the clock.

'Just five more minutes'

I started this chapter thinking about Sonnyboy, who demonstrated a relationship to the clock that was more closely related to his cultural background than the timetabled practices in his classroom. My interview participants reflected on insights they had gained about differences between their own and young children's relationship with time:

> Their sense of time I feel in a way in early childhood is much more experiential . . . their actual experience of time is very distinct from adults and it's quite hard for adults to understand when everything is timed, when we have so many items on our persons that tell the time . . . Everything is timetables, and schedules and the timetables in school are provided by the adults. They are for the adults, first and foremost. I think that all these kind of structures that we have as adults to help us understand time are not the way that young children experience time.
>
> I think it's much more about, if young children are excited about something then I think that they probably experience time quite quickly and that things are flowing but if they are having to wait for something that's good, they experience the time quite slowly. I think if they're doing something boring, then obviously that drags time down and for real slow experience. Food, hunger and excitement and fear, I think that these emotions probably have more of an effect on young children's sense of time, than the numbers that we attribute to the minutes.
>
> *(William Clark, interview, October 2020)*

The physicist Carlo Rovelli emphasises this experiential dimension to time, describing how time is not a fixed concept but is experienced and narrated in different ways: 'Time is elastic in our personal experience of it. Hours fly by like minutes and minutes are oppressively slow, as if they were centuries' (2018: 52).

Canning (2019), in her ethnographic study of the social play of young children in community based 'stay and play' sessions noted how children, parents and early childhood educators narrated their sense of time:

> Just 5 more minutes!' was a common phrase used by all, but with very different meanings. Children used it to gain more play, pleading with adults for extra time; educators used it as a warning that the daily routine of events was moving on, and parents used it almost as a reward, giving their child and their playmates extra time.
>
> *(Canning 2019: 11)*

Canning shows how different understandings of time or temporalities can occur simultaneously in ECEC, even when the same phrase is spoken. The management of time is a powerful tool. Extra time can be seen as desired, or a means of control or reward. So for young children engaged in play, more time was a desired outcome that needed to be argued for. 'Just 5 more minutes' from an educator's perspective here can be seen as an exercise of control and for parents too where the power to give or withhold time for play remains with the adult.

Conclusion

The relationship with time is embedded within early childhood education – and often has remained implicit and taken for granted. Time has 'currency' and can be a precious commodity. I have begun to look in this chapter at relating to the clock, as one significant aspect of thinking about time in learning environments with young children. Thinking about the close bond between schooling and the clock has roots associated with a factory system of learning and the industrial revolution. Here is an example of a timepiece from a textile mill in England, documented by the textile artist Claire Wellesley-Smith in her book about 'Slow stitch' (2015):

> In some workplaces, there were even clocks made that measured productivity as time: a two-faced timepiece in a Preston silk factory was connected to a watermill that powered the machinery. The first clock face showed the time while the second showed 'lost time' if the wheel did not turn quickly enough, and this time had to be made up at the end of the working day.
>
> *(Wellesley-Smith 2015: 22)*

I find this a striking image. Productivity and 'lost time' may not be measured on a two-faced timepiece in schools and early childhood provision but is the pressure there nevertheless? This raises questions about whose time is being lost – that of adults or children? And lost from what? I continue this thinking in Chapter 3 by focusing on 'Play time'.

Questions

1 What examples have you encountered in education where future goals have 'foreshadowed' the present moment?
2 To what extent do you think fear of being judged by others plays in a hurried early childhood practice?
3 How would you illustrate the difference between time policies and time practices?

Notes

1 The Reception class is the first compulsory year of schooling in maintained schools in England and Wales for children between four and five years old.
2 Key Stage One children in maintained schools in England and Wales are between five and seven years and Key Stage Two children are between seven and 11 years.
3 Reading Recovery is a specialist reading programme developed by the New Zealand educator Marie Clay (1993, 2019).

3
PLAY TIME

Introduction

What can the concept of play tell us about a different way of engaging with time and what language can help us do so? There are two parts to the chapter. The first focuses on play and time and the second part identifies the concepts of 'stretched time' and 'timefullness' that we can see happening when children play and are embedded in slow practices.

This discussion is set within the contemporary frame of the importance of play in uncertain times.

The topic of play has appeared and reappeared in national debate at different stages of the pandemic (for example, Grant 2021). Taking the UK as an example, this included photographs of locked playgrounds appearing in the media as an indication of Covid restrictions introduced during the first lockdown. Play then became a topic about what learning in lockdown should look like. Kate Pahl made the case for the value of play in an opinion piece titled: 'Play is educational too: an alternative look at learning during lockdown':

> Literacy practices are lived. Children make meaning from all kinds of things: from tissue paper, pens, paper, blankets, toys, processions of objects, and their meaning making is not confined to words. Rolling, jumping and running are all part of meaning making . . . . Children make tissue paper birds, they create treasure trails using maps and pieces of paper, they bounce about on the sofa while wrestling. Children sing, dance and whoop while watching television or playing games – they create things in response to online adventures, such as the 'floss' dance craze.
> . . . Most importantly, this time is an opportunity to do nothing. Day dreaming, lying around, thinking, all these are important parts of being.
>
> *(Pahl 2020)*

DOI: 10.4324/9781003051626-4

This description brings alive the different rhythms of children's play, including the very physical to the moments of stillness: 'daydreaming, lying around, thinking'.

Pahl's articulation of the value of play in the pandemic was in sharp contrast to a new kind of hurriedness that some children appeared to experience where the busyness of school and keeping up with school routines was replaced with a different kind of hurriedness – a fully timetabled schedule of activities, online and offline.

As public discourse began to think about life beyond the pandemic play again featured in debate. Nicholas Tampio, writing in *The Washington Post* in February 2021, after almost a year of the pandemic, underlined the importance of play: 'This Summer governments, civil society and families should look for ways to give children a chance to do activities that are voluntary, joyful and imaginative: that is, to play' (Tampio 2021).

Tampio, as a political scientist, was one voice among many from different disciplines who have advocated for the value of play for children in uncertain times. In England there was a call for a 'summer filled with play' to recover from the pandemic. Helen Dodd, Professor of Child Psychology comments: 'Children need time to reconnect and play with their friends, they need to be reminded how good it feels to be outdoors after so long inside and they need to get physically active again.' Paediatricians joined in this campaign. Michael Absoud, a consultant in neurodisability at Evelina Children's hospital in London, expressed concern about the decline or absence of opportunities to socialise for children with special needs: '. . . the loss of social play is really a worry. It's been a year now, that's significant in a six-year-old's life. Play is important for the developing brain, it's how children learn, I would prescribe play if I could' (*The Guardian*, 14 February, 2021).

Set against this background I will turn to temporal dimensions to thinking about play, firstly by thinking about how play by its very nature challenges a time-bound educational system.

Secondly, I explore briefly some of the explicit and implicit relationships with time and rhythm discussed by Friedrich Froebel (Liebschner, 1992) in conceptualising kindergartens.

Next, we will discuss key terms in thinking about play and time: 'stretched time' and 'timefullness'. The words we use to think about time matters. Exploring the vocabulary available can make explicit ways of relating to time that for the most part are assumed and not articulated. This 'bringing to the surface' may reveal some of the hidden layers of tensions and ambiguities behind policies, principles and practices.

Lastly we consider whose time counts in relation to play?

The paradox of play, school and the relationship with time

Play needs time to breathe and by its very nature play is unscripted or else I think it will cease to be play. Scotland's Play Strategy emphasises this open-ended nature of play:

> Play encompasses children's behaviour which is freely chosen, personally directed and intrinsically motivated. It is performed for no external goal or

reward and is a fundamental and integral part of healthy development – not only for individual children but also for the society in which we live.

(Scottish Government 2013: 12)

This quality of the open-endedness of play poses perhaps its biggest challenge to a measurement culture in education. ECEC contexts that support a play-based peda-gogy are similarly an uncomfortable fit with a policy emphasis on school readiness and assessment. The irony is, as Murris and Kohan (2021) remind us, the original meaning of the Greek word 'schole' was free-time or leisure, rest or ease. Kate Cowan reflected during her interview on the tensions she experienced between her own Post-graduate certificate of education (PGCE) training (2007–2008) and her experience of practice:

> I think it's really challenging because . . . there's deeply held beliefs about early childhood education and pedagogy often and of how children learn, around play and exploration outdoors, hands on learning. I think they sit in tension with the policy especially around school readiness and assessment. What is seen as worth measuring in those assessments don't always marry up with these ideas that have a really long history as well. Froebel, Montessori, Susan Isaacs and others. They're part of the fabric and weave of our history in this country and part of my training certainly. It really valued those sorts of early childhood pedagogies and taught us in depth about them and then when you're in the classroom context it can feel a little bit disjointed in that you're trying to marry them up with the expectations.
>
> I think that's particularly the case for early years settings in schools. So Reception classes in particular and nurseries that are part of primary schools because I think to keep that early years identity and ethos and work to the Early years Foundation Stage[1] (EYFS) when the rest of the school is working to the National Curriculum can be a bit of a challenge potentially and the early years ends up becoming more 'schoolified', as a result. I think it's really tricky for practitioners because that they are asked to do so much.

(Kate Cowan, interview, July 2020)

Kate Cowan is discussing the tensions she has experienced between the post grad-uate teaching training she received in England in 2007–2008 and witnessing a 'schoolification' (Bradbury 2019) of ECEC in practice particularly when the early years provision is happening within a primary school environment. This 'readying' for school is embedded in the Early Years Foundation Stage framework that applies to children in schools and other early years provision in England:

> The EYFS framework sets the statutory standards for the development, learning and care of children from birth to age 5. The EYFS framework sets the standards that all early years providers, including schools with early years provision, must meet to ensure that children learn and develop well and are kept healthy and safe. It promotes teaching and learning to ensure children's

'school readiness' and gives children the broad range of knowledge and skills that provide the right foundation for good future progress through school and life.

(Department for Education 2021: 5)

This returns us to the discussion about a forward driven or proleptic approach (Jewitt and Jones 2005) in Chapter 2, where preparation for the next stage overshadows the present.

Mara Krechevsky and colleagues at Project Zero, at Harvard University point to an underlying tension between the concept of play and the relationship with the clock in school in what the team identify as: 'the paradox between the timeless nature of play and the timetabled nature of school' (Krechevsky et al. 2019: 71). This has been one of the issues discussed in the Pedagogy of Play project, a collaboration between Project Zero (Harvard) and the Lego Foundation to investigate in a systematic way playful learning and teaching in school (Mardell et al. 2016). The project began by working with the International School of Billund in Denmark and has subsequently expanded to additional international research sites.

Mara explained further in her interview:

> We were working with a school in Denmark. The middle school teachers decided that in order to really have kids feel a responsibility for their own learning you needed to rethink this concept of time and so they decided to do an experiment where they removed the timetable for a few weeks, and students were able to compose their own schedules. Teachers were available for help but kids could choose where and when to study. One of the observations, of a student I was following was that, because the time was up to him, it allowed for more opportunity for flow because he was able to pursue a path that he was interested in [whereas] in the regular timetable he wouldn't have had the time to continue researching this unusual thing . . . It probably doesn't work for all students, but I think that it was a bold and brave experiment that the teachers carried out and to the best of my knowledge, they are continuing with the student–composed schedule twice a year.
>
> *(Mara Krechevsky, interview, October 2020)*

The project identified eight key principles of a pedagogy of play of which the eighth principle is of particular relevance to the focus of this chapter:

> 8. Collectively studying the paradoxes between play and school. Fostering playful learning entails *navigating a set of paradoxes between the nature of play and the nature of school*. Collaborative and systematic study of artifacts of student learning (documentation), can help educators navigate these paradoxes.
>
> *(Krechevsky et al. 2019: 74)*

One of the paradoxes are made explicit in this principle, rather than being ignored. Engaging with pedagogical documentation is seen as a way of addressing this tension. We will be looking further at the significance of pedagogical documentation as a slow practice in Chapter 7.

Next we step back to look briefly at what Friedrich Froebel (1782–1852), the creator of the first kindergarten, and his ideas about play and freedom (for example, Froebel 1867; Liebschner 1992; Brosterman 1997; Bruce 1991, 2016, 2017, 2020; Tovey 2017) can contribute to a re-examination of the relationship with time in contemporary ECEC.

Froebel, play and freedom

There are two sides to freedom, what it prevents you experiencing (freedom from) and what it allows you to do. Liebscher explains Froebel's articulation of freedom **from** a formal method of transmissive education and freedom **for** children to participate fully in their own learning:

> Both these notions of freedom from something, **freedom from** rote learning and freedom from inappropriate teaching led Froebel to a more positive notion of freedom, namely **freedom for** children to participate, to choose, to act, to observe, to play and above all *to be allowed time to absorb new knowledge at their own speed of learning.*
>
> *(Liebschner 1992: 66)*

There is an interesting link with the Slow Movement principles here of a 'tempo giusto' or balance that Honoré describes (Honoré 2004). Froebel emphasises the importance of children being able to learn at their own speed. The temporal dimension is highlighted here. Opportunities are created for children to take on board new ideas and absorb, or make connections with, their existing webs of knowledge. Freedom to play is central to this process. This is in contrast to what Jarvis has called 'an acceleration curriculum' (2020: 42–50) with heavy age-related demands on young children and assessment.

Tina Bruce has drawn on her extensive reading and writing about Froebel's teaching to describe 12 features characterising a Froebelian approach to childhood play (Bruce 2020). I have chosen four of these characteristics to indicate some of the many strands of the relationship between play and time.

> Free flow play actively uses direct, firsthand experiences, which draw on the child's powerful inner drive to struggle, manipulate materials, explore, discover and practise over and over again.
>
> *(Bruce 2020)*

This characteristic acknowledges that children in self-directed play may return repeatedly to the same ideas, stories and tasks they have set themselves to practice. Practitioners who took part in the focus group to discuss the initial findings of my study commented on how even after several months of being at home due to the pandemic some children returned to play they had been absorbed in before lockdown. It raises the question, is such play seen as a problem and 'time to move on' or is revisiting play supported and valued?

> Play is an active process without an end product. When the play fades, so does its tangibility. It can never again be replayed in exactly the same way. It is of the moment and vanishes when the play episode ends. This aids flexibility of thought and the adaptability central to the intellectual life of the child.
>
> *(Bruce 2020)*

The ephemeral nature of play may be one of the reasons play can pose a challenge to an educational system that emphasises measurement and testing. In drawing attention to these qualities Bruce refers to the relationship with time again here. An open-ended process is by its nature not primarily driven by the clock. How long an episode of play will take cannot necessarily be prescribed in advance. This raises questions about how much flexibility is there to adjust routines around play and what impact do timetables have on young children's experiences of ECEC?

> Play is about wallowing in ideas, feelings and relationships and the prowess of the physical body. It helps the process of becoming aware of self in relation to others and the universe. It brings unity and interconnectedness.
>
> *(Bruce 2020)*

The choice of the word 'wallowing' suggests taking your time. These are not rushed activities dominated by clock time but experiences where immersion is made possible. There is also a sense of enjoyment. Perhaps this is why the word might seem provocative in a professional context. Maybe it is the case in some early childhood environments that the pressures to be seen to perform and to be busy have squeezed out a sense of fun?

> Play is an integrating mechanism which brings together everything the child has been learning, knows and understands. It is rooted in real experience that it processes and explores. It is self healing in most situations and brings an intellectual life that is self aware, connected to others, community and the world beyond. Early childhood play becomes a powerful resource for life both in the present and the future.
>
> *(Bruce 2020)*

If young children have the opportunity for unscripted, uninterrupted play, Froebel claimed that this would enable children to make connections with what they already knew. This is the key Froebelian principle of 'connectedness' where children are able to link 'different domains of experience and make sense of the new in relation to what is already known' (Tovey 2017: 38). There is a strong temporal dimension to this understanding of connectedness. If children are supported to connect to their existing experiences, this acknowledges that children have a past with knowledge to bring to new encounters. Liz Brooker (2002) demonstrated how young children may or may not have such opportunities to make such connections on starting school, if their previous knowledge and experiences are undervalued, dismissed or undiscovered (and see Chapter 10). Helen Tovey's explanation of contemporary applications of Froebelian principles are helpful in relation to play and time. Tovey identifies the availability of time as a key feature of a Froebelian environment as stated in the epigraph at the start of this chapter:

> Froebelian educators create long periods of open-ended, uninterrupted time so that both children and adults can become deeply involved in play and other learning activities. Time is not 'filled' but is freed from all unnecessary interruptions.
>
> *(Tovey 2017: 42)*

The phrase 'uninterrupted time' leads us into the next section where I consider language to describe the unique relationship between play and time that have wider implications for understanding slow practices.

Stretched time and 'timefullness'

Finding the vocabulary to articulate alternative ways of relating to the clock may make it easier to recognise where these practices are already happening in ECEC and raise possibilities of how to increase these experiences for young children.

Stretched time

Harriet Cuffaro (1995) gives a detailed account of working with John Dewey's ideas in an early childhood 'classroom' (to use Cuffaro's term). On reading and rereading Cuffaro's book I am left with a strong impression of the unhurried culture within this space. Cuffaro describes the importance of creating opportunities for uninterrupted time or as she describes, 'nonfragmented stretches of time' or my favourite term, 'stretched time':

> With such awareness and understanding it becomes important to think about a schedule that makes it possible for children to work without many interruptions and transitions from one activity to another.
>
> Nonfragmented stretches of time not only give children the opportunity for more in-depth involvement and experimentation, but also allow room for situations to evolve, to become meaningful in a way that they may not be at first-glance. Within this stretched time, greater possibility exists for making choices and for experiencing the consequences of one's doing. Such an

approach requires that time be viewed as perspective, as rhythm, as opportunity, and that the present moment be fully valued.

(Cuffaro 1995: 42)

Cuffaro emphasises in this description what her approach to time makes possible. It opens up opportunities for children to, for example, make choices and then see what happens as a result. Enabling young children to demonstrate such agency requires time and patience on the part of the adults (Oliveira-Formosinho and de Sousa 2019). We will return to the idea of patience in Chapter 11. There seems to me a close link between 'time freed' and the phrases 'nonfragmented time' and 'stretched time' – children are given the opportunity for more prolonged engagement – moving beyond the 'first glance'.

There may be many reasons why young children can find their time in ECEC divided into shorter and shorter fragments of play. This was one of the contrasts Mary Jane Drummond noticed in her reflections on reading the detailed accounts by Susan Isaacs about Malting House school:

> in comparison with the primary classrooms where I have taught in the past and regularly observe today, there was, no time wasted in the business of forming into lines, waiting in lines, completing the registers, collecting lunch money, searching for PE equipment all the events that add up to evaporated time in Campbell's vivid phrase (Campbell and Neill 1994: 23). All the available time was available for the children, not for the teachers' routines; it was filled with the children's dramatic, vivid lives.
>
> *(2000: 3)*

Drummond refers to Campbell and Neill's term here of 'evaporated time' as a concept of time experienced by both children and adults. There were several moments in my research study Living Spaces (Clark 2010a) where four- and five-year-old children conveyed to me periods of 'evaporated time' during their day including time spent in circle time on the 'scratchy carpet' and waiting in line for lunch in the school dinner hall (2010a: 49–81).

There may be a connection between thinking about children's opportunities for 'stretched time' to play and Deleuze and Guattari's concepts of 'smooth' and 'striated' space, bringing constructs about space into considerations of time underline the interconnections between the temporal and the spatial. Deleuze and Guattari (2004) introduce the process of quilting alongside other models for exploring ways of thinking. My understanding of a smooth space is one which is playful, offering the opportunity for open-ended exploration and improvisation, as demonstrated in a 'crazy' quilt where scraps of material can be assembled in a free-style way without following a pattern:

> A smooth space or nomad space gives freedom in which to act in unconstrained or unscripted ways (Hansen et al. 2017) and can give rise to nomadic

thinking. Olsson describes how this 'thinking not only deconstructs codes and habits but actually connects them in new and unexpected ways' (2009: 25). A striated or sedentary space comes with a pre-defined narrative but as in the history of the quilt, as Deleuze and Guattari describe, there is a relationship between the striated and the smooth.

(Clark 2019b: 240)

I would like to continue in this section to introduce different vocabulary that makes explicit alternative relationships to time in education. Povey et al. (2021) discuss 'regulated time' and 'expansive time' in relation to the teaching of mathematics in primary schools in England. Whilst they acknowledge criticism of drawing attention to binaries, Povey and colleagues make the case for identifying different constructs of time in the classroom in order to make this temporal dimension more explicit and therefore open to change. They draw on the social theory of timescapes (Adam 2000):

Timescape points to the complex and overlapping dimensions of time that include physical time and subjective experiences of time – human time (Schatzki 2006; Compton-Lilly 2015). It acknowledges the multidimensional, recursive, non-linear lived experience of time.

(Povey et al. 2021: 120)

Thinking with 'timescapes' makes space for acknowledging the experiential dimensions to time alongside the linear, timetabled, clock time. Povey et al. (2021) make the case for 'regulated time' as being identified with neoliberal schooling practices:

The neutral, decontextualised empty time of calendars and clocks [which] remains the unquestioned medium and the parameter within which . . . activities are experienced, constructed, recorded and commodified.

(Adam 2000: 126 cited in Povey et al. 2021: 121)

Teaching that adopts 'expansive time' is prepared to make room for the unexpected and 'unfinishedness' where children can continue to build on and return to ideas. Drawing on the work of the curriculum theorist David Jardine, expansive time can be seen as 'worthwhile time' (2008, 2012, 2013). Jardine asks:

What makes some experiences worthy of rest and repose, worthy of returning, worthy of tarrying and remembering, of taking time, of whiling away our lives in their presence?

(2008: n.p)

We will return to these ideas of stretched or expansive timescapes in subsequent chapters, as we consider what slow practices in ECEC look and feel like.

Timefullness

I have discussed at the start of this chapter how play enables a different relationship with time. The language we use can help articulate what is happening in taking a less hurried approach in ECEC. I think the concept of 'timefullness' is helpful to consider in this context. I have come across this term from two very different disciplinary perspectives.

Becoming friends of time

The theologian John Swinton in his book *Becoming friends of time* discusses time and disability. He describes the time of the clock as being assumed to be linear, dynamic, forward facing, measurable and controllable (2016: 22–23). Taking a theological perspective Swinton challenges the tyranny of the clock and proposes an expansive view of time that is in tune with how time is experienced and lived. This opens up a discussion about the relationship between time and ethics, drawing attention to the value bases sometimes implicit in the relationship with time. On a global scale, the imposition of linear Eurocentric notions of time can be understood as part of a colonial legacy that challenged more indigenous modes of time (Shahjahan 2015; Murris and Kohan 2021).

Thinking about time, practices and relationships raises questions about what is seen to be a good life for children and for adults? Swinton draws on the following observation from Bader-Saye: 'the ways we experience, name and interpret time contribute to the kinds of communities we imagine and inhabit' (Badyer-Saye 2006: 96 in Swinton 2016: 63). This draws attention to thinking about the different ways in which time is experienced, including for the youngest children in ECEC and for children with disabilities. Swinton argues that in engaging deeply with people who experience time differently it can change our own perceptions of time and we can learn to live in new ways.

'Becoming friends with time' suggests to me not being trapped by time or escaping time (timelessness) but of establishing a different relationship. In thinking with Swinton it makes explicit the spiritual dimension to reconsidering how we relate to the clock and about what is prioritised. The concept of timefullness links to the Froebelian idea of time freed, discussed earlier. This expansive view of time underlines the human and humane dimension to these discussions. It alerts us to the importance of our own personal histories in relation to how we value time, in the same way as I have discussed how the pandemic has impacted differently on individuals' and families' sense of time. During my interviews there were several moments when the personal nature of these inquiries about time became evident. I refer to two observations from Sylvia Kind here.

ALISON: So, what can slow look like? When you first read this, what did you think about? . . . what are the slow practices that you've come across in your own or others research interests and practice?

SYLVIA: To me, I think, I wouldn't necessarily have always called it slow but that is the way I work. And it really, to me, has its roots, not just in what I read but in my own early childhood experiences, to a beautiful Montessori School where one of my teachers she retired when she was 90 years old studied under Maria Montessori, and they had a full time art teacher, and it was on a couple acres right by the beach and so we would do our Montessori work in the morning so that the afternoons were extended times outside painting at the beach, learning about the birds. So, that is always ingrained in me as a way of being an education. And I was there from preschool through elementary years through grade three. And so it's not just what I read I think it's also what I experienced.

(Sylvia Kind, interview, November 2020)

We see in Sylvia's reflection how her early childhood experiences of education had a particular relationship with time, informed by a Montessorian approach that has had a deep impact on what she views education is about. Sylvia continued:

probably and quite honestly, my best teacher in this has been my son Nathanial who was born with multiple disabilities and is nonverbal. Learning to walk to his rhythm, to notice the things he notices, and to learn his language and his diverse ways of communicating, of experiencing, and of being in this world, and his unique ways of attending to things, has shaped me more than anyone's research.

Learning to walk to Nathaniel's rhythm illustrates what a timefull approach can look like with a different relationship to the clock. This is one in which it is recognised as Swinton comments 'each body holds its own time and each task moves to its own rhythm. Each task completed is the product of steady, purposeful, timefull action rather than frenzied, time-deprived drives for efficiency' (Swinton 2016: 71).

The second understanding of the concept of timefullness I have come across is in work by the geologist Marcia Bjornerud (2018) who makes the case for a stretched view of time that is more able to take a longer view of history and to take concerns seriously for the future of the planet. She challenges the appeal of things being unchanging or 'timeless' and instead makes the case for our sense of time to be more aligned with geological time:

So the call for timefulness[sic] is to acknowledge that we are temporal creatures, to learn something about the history of the Earth and the environment in which we are deeply embedded and with which we have evolved. And to learn to anticipate the ways that our actions as humans, who are increasingly numerous, will interact with the unfolding natural processes in ways that may not be what we would like them to be.

(Bjornerud and Claus 2018, unpaginated https://humansandnature.org/
timefulness-interview-with-marcia-bjornerud/)

Maybe it is not too surprising to find theologians and geologists to be among those to be discussing the importance of time. Both disciplines take the longer view. They are interested more in the flow of time over centuries than in clock time. Both disciplines caution against short term thinking.

I will continue to refer to the concepts of 'stretched time' and 'timefullness' and the related terms discussed here in the following chapters as they seem to me to encapsulate an alternative relationship to time than the hurried, tightly timetabled and time-poor accounts discussed earlier.

Conclusion

Play has been the starting point in this chapter for discussing alternative relationships with time in education and ECEC in particular. Tensions and paradoxes have emerged between the underlying characteristics of play and the timeframes within which education operates across the age range. These tensions relate to questions about the purpose of education and what is seen as of value or to use Jardine's phrase 'worthwhile' (2008). Such questions have become more intense in recent periods of global uncertainty and can be seen in post-pandemic discussions about future priorities for education. The relationship with time is an often implicit thread in such debates. This chapter has raised alternative ways of relating to the clock that are relevant for ECEC, as well to other sectors of education. Thinking about play gives us a window on a timefull, expansive or stretched approach to time. This suggests why the early childhood field has so much to offer in terms of reimagining the unhurried child that this chapter has only begun to explore. I will expand in more detail in the next chapter in the search for definitions of slow pedagogies and slow knowledge.

Questions

1   To what extent do you agree or disagree with the idea that there is a 'paradox between the timeless nature of play and the timetabled nature of school?' (Krechevsky et al. 2019: 71).
2   What does 'time freed' look like for young children in your context?
3   What examples of 'stretched time' and 'evaporated time' have you come across involving young children?

Note

1   Children in a Reception class in a primary school in England follow the Early Years Foundation Stage Curriculum. Children in Year One begin the first year of the National Curriculum. Different national early years frameworks exist across the UK. The Foundation Phase framework in Wales will be replaced by Curriculum for Wales in September 2022. In Scotland 'Curriculum for excellence' is the national curriculum for 3- to 18-year-olds. Realising the Ambition (2020) is the national practice guidance for early years in Scotland.

4
SLOW PEDAGOGIES AND SLOW KNOWLEDGE

Introduction

I set out in this chapter to draw together ideas about the common characteristics of a slow pedagogy in early childhood education and what slow knowledge in this context looks like. I refer to slow pedagogies in the plural in the chapter title as this exploration is not about outlining a one-size template. This has been a meaning making process with my research participants and in subsequent discussions with others following my presentations of initial findings. The interviews were dialogues, designed with the intention of creating opportunities for us to think out loud together about our understandings of how the concept of 'slow' pedagogies and slow knowledge connected with our experiences of early childhood teacher education, research and practice.

I start by considering the concept of a slow pedagogy of place.

A slow pedagogy

The concept of a 'slow pedagogy of place' has emerged from environmental/outdoor education (Payne and Wattchow 2009) connecting the values of the Slow movement with approaches to teaching about our relationship with the planet. Payne and Wattchow make the case for countering what they describe as 'take-away pedagogies': 'fast, take-away, virtual, globalized, downloadable uptake versions of electronic pedagogy – a technology or technics of increasingly abstracted experience' (Payne 2006 in Payne and Wattchow 2009: 17). There is an echo here of the Slow food movement's campaigning against a standardised take-away food culture. Take-away pedagogies might offer an easily accessible, uniform product but is there longer-term nourishment? A similar point was raised in my interview with Júlia Oliveira-Formosino about early childhood practice that relied on worksheets:

DOI: 10.4324/9781003051626-5

> A worksheet is quicker, one after the other, one for language, one for maths. . . . But then, it is quick but is it helpful? Is it going to be in children's memory? What children learn with worksheets, is it going to be so deep and so durable?
>
> *(Júlia Oliveira-Formosinho, interview, October 2020)*

Payne and Wattchow (2009) call for a deconstruction and reconstruction of fast pedagogies: 'A slow or ecopedagogy, allows us to pause or dwell in spaces for more than a fleeting moment and, therefore, encourages us to attach and receive meaning from that place' (2009: 15). Thinking about both the temporal and spatial are brought together through the module they developed for environmental education undergraduates: 'Experiencing the Australian Landscape' that I have discussed elsewhere (Clark 2020: 140–141). Payne and Wattchow take their students away from disembodied, second-hand learning, opening up the opportunity for repeated immersion in the same coastal environment. No one else can take your place in this kind of learning. It is experienced and reflected upon firsthand, in depth and engaging the senses in keeping with a phenomenological approach to pedagogy as van Manen explains:

> Phenomenology can be adopted to explore the unique meanings of any pedagogical experience or phenomenon, such as the experience of care, recognition, patience, encouragement, hope, respect, humbleness, and so forth. The practical significance of phenomenological pedagogy is the thoughtfulness and tact it affords in pedagogical situations and relations.
>
> *(2016: 40)*

We will see these theoretical strands reappearing across this chapter and through the book as I explore different slow practices where the influence of phenomenological ideas and embodied learning reappears, whether for example, thinking about outdoor experiences, in everyday routines or in exploring materials.

Thinking about the slow pedagogy of place has been one way in for thinking explicitly about slow in early childhood education, as Kari-Anne Jørgensen-Vittersø explained:

> I got to know the ideas about slow pedagogies and Payne because I'm also working with outdoor education. I think it connects to some of the aspects I identified when I did my PhD. It's the sensory aspect, multi-sensory aspect. It is the identity of place and the possibility for moving and dwelling and connecting to place. And not just space but to place. And it also connects to how we see time, if we just see it as a chronological time. And I think actually to be able to practice slow pedagogies and to understand some of the content of it you have to stay with children over a longer period of time. So maybe in the ways we are doing research we don't really see it.
>
> *(Kari-Anne Jørgensen-Vittersø, interview, October 2020)*

I was interested to find out how my research participants would relate to the concept of a 'slow pedagogy'. I had invited each to take part as I had observed what I understood to be 'slow practices' in their research and practice with young children or in their approaches to early childhood teacher education. I did not know however whether they would recognise the concept, how they might define slow pedagogies and what ideas, theories or people had influenced their thinking. In Kari-Anne's response we see a strong link with the 'slow pedagogy of place' drawing on her experience in outdoor education and an emphasis on the multi-sensory aspects of such encounters (for example, Jørgensen 2016). This was an unfamiliar term to the majority of my other study participants, but their pedagogical approaches could each be seen in different ways to contribute to understanding what slow pedagogies in ECEC can look like and how to make explicit the underpinning values.

There are three interconnected themes that emerged from these discussions: 'Being with', 'Going off track' and 'Diving deep.'

'Being with'

> It is this idea of 'being with' I think that would be the essence of a slow pedagogy and that 'being with' isn't always slow in terms of time, again, there could be intensities and vibrancies and things erupting. It's finding the rhythm of the children you're working with, the adults you are working with, the materials you're working with. [It's] how do we be with others, be with ideas, not just as if we stand outside of it . . . to me I guess it was this idea of 'being with'.
>
> *(Sylvia Kind, interview, November 2020)*

Sylvia Kind is an instructor and researcher based at Capilano University, Vancouver in Canada. Sylvia's definition of a slow pedagogy encapsulates the idea of an experiential and relational pedagogy where the emphasis is on engagement between the teacher, children and the environment. This is not a transmissive pedagogy (Oliveira-Formosinho and de Sousa 2019) where the teacher remains in control of a predefined content of knowledge and how it is conveyed. The concept of 'being with' is linked to finding the rhythm of the children but also attention to the 'rhythm' of colleagues, materials and ideas. We will see what this kind of attunement can look like in the following chapters.

Sylvia continues by describing what 'being with' looks and feels like in her children's studio, a small room adjacent to the campus childcare provision at Capilano University (Kind et al. 2019):

> In studio work with children, particularly, that's the biggest thing that I'm working on always is cultivating a culture of thinking together and working together that isn't something you can implement, it is something that can only be cultivated over time.

> It's not about teaching a child what to do rather cultivating a space where we're helping each other notice, working together, borrowing each other's ideas, noticing others, working with somebody else's ideas instead of just assuming that everybody has their own ideas –it's their idea, their image, their proposition but, once it's in the studio it belongs to everybody. We can all engage with it. That cultivating a way of being together and thinking together to me is the primary work, even though all kinds of other artistic things happen and there might be other ideas but that's the foundation of it all. Without that I don't think we could do very much.
>
> *(Sylvia Kind, interview, November 2020)*

Sylvia's response makes explicit the relationship with time that is involved. This is about 'cultivating a culture of thinking together.' Cultivation takes time. Sylvia then brings together the idea of cultivation and collaboration. This links directly to Froebel's conceptualisation of a kindergarten as a place of growth: the children's garden (see Chapter 3).

Tahmina, who has studied and written with Sylvia about her experiences as an early childhood student (Kind et al. 2019) and now is a colleague, explains further how these ideas tie together for her with a definition of a slow pedagogy:

> I would connect a slow pedagogy with a pedagogy of listening from Rinaldi, pedagogy of thoughtfulness and tactfulness from van Manen. Van Manen talks about being a thoughtful and tactful educator. I would also connect it with Aoki's concept of lingering and dwelling and with the practice of A/r/tography . . . . Lingering in places and really being in and attending to things, paying attention to things, and being in a way that you're not there to do something, but rather to be and listen. Because you're really slowing down. Sometimes as educators we are so pressured to always do something . . . as if we have to be productive. [It's about] setting aside that productive machine and thinking about, 'what can my own 'ways of being' do? what can it invite? and how might we be able to become much more attuned to things as we slow down and as we listen, and as we inquire into things?'
>
> *(Tahmina Shayman, interview, November 2020)*

There are several important strands about 'being with' in Tahmina's response. I will discuss two here, 'lingering' and 'listening', and will return to these themes in subsequent chapters. Sylvia and Tahmina both draw on the work of teacher and curriculum theorist Ted Aoki (Pinar and Irwin 2005; Magrini 2015; Lee et al. 2022) whose writing and speaking has had wide influence in curriculum studies, beginning in Canada (Pinar 2005). The concept of 'lingering' in Aoki's writing is deeply connected with listening. He held the idea of 'curriculum as planned' together with the importance of understanding 'curriculum as lived'– how the curriculum is experienced by children and students and connected or not with their lived experience of the world. 'Aoki asks me to listen' as Rajabali comments about working with Aoki's ideas (Rajabali, 2022: 41). This approach to listening views the pedagogical relationship as 'a holistic activity of the total person – head, heart and lifestyle, all as one' (Aoki 1983/2005: 116). This is an approach to pedagogy that is unafraid to aim to bring 'love, joy and beauty and even laughter, to the lives we contact in this imperfect world' (Grimmett 2022: 157).

I am struck, having been introduced to Aoki's work through this research study, how pertinent his ideas seem to be when reconsidering the relationship with time in ECEC. Lee et al. (2022) make explicit this connection:

> In many ways, Aokian scholarship is slow scholarship, because 'contemplative lingering gives time. It widens the being that is more than being-active. When life regains its capacity for contemplation, it gains in time and space, in duration and vast-ness' (Han 2017: 113). Lingering grants an opening for pause, breath, an experience of duration, and a deepening of time so that wisdom can grace one's presence.
>
> *(Lee et al. 2022: 4)*

The opportunity to see 'being' as more than just 'being-active' offers an expansive view of time that establishes a way of being comfortable with pauses, not needing to always move on to the next thing. Tahmina has reflected with her fellow early childhood student, Cheryl Cameron, about 'learning to linger':

> Lingering to us, meant being loosened from routines and conventions, taking up the unexpected, dwelling with questions and curiosities, seeing from an aesthetic perspective, and fully entering into an emergent living or lived curriculum (see also May 2000).
>
> *(Kind et al. 2019: 72)*

We can also see in Tahmina's reflection the close links between the concept of 'being with' and listening as expressed in the 'pedagogy of listening' (Rinaldi 2005, 2006). Carlina Rinaldi was the former director of the municipal early childhood centres in Reggio Emilia, in Northern Italy where she succeeded Loris Malaguzzi (see Chapter 7 and 11). When Rinaldi describes how an early childhood centre can be a site for 'multiple listening' this can be understood as different forms of 'being with' children, colleagues, parents, the environment and ideas. This openness to experiences and perspectives is time-consuming and underlines the unhurried nature of these encounters and takes us back to the concept of slow. We will return to these ideas drawn from the early childhood programme of Reggio Emilia in subsequent chapters (see Chapter 7 and 11).

I am drawn to a way of thinking about ECEC where there is time to 'be with' children's ideas, where there is time to listen to the unexpected and the urgent concerns. Kate Cowan expressed this shared belief about a slow pedagogy:

> I think it's seeing learning as something that you do *with* children, rather than to children, and . . . that has time for wonder and uncertainty. And then that changes the adults' role so the adults' role is then about presenting possibilities for inquiry and tools to support these rather than . . . having a goal in mind and . . . progressing children along that way.
>
> *(Kate Cowan, interview, July 2020)*

I end this section with an account from my interview with Júlia Oliveira-Formosinho who gave an example of the ability of an educator to 'be with' and 'stay with' children's enquiries through project work:

> For instance in project work when children . . . 'Oh Helia? how was this baby born . . . ?' So all the environment Ellia the teacher created about listening was important too, because the other little boy said 'okay I'm interested in that as well' and the other said 'okay but my mother is going to be upset. So what should we do? Should we ask parents if they want to help us in learning about this topic?' So all this requires time. Listening to questions or registering the questions reading questions back to children for them to say yes that's what I asked, not what you asked. Now let's write the letter A letter to parents to see if they can help us . . . . And so then writing to parents and reading with children, their answers of help. This is a real case. She's a doctor. And she says, Oh that's so good as a doctor maybe I can help so then they have the help of a mother, that was at the same time a medical doctor and so on.
>
> *(Júlia Oliveira-Formosinho, interview, October 2020)*

We can see in this example the deep respect for children's ideas and concerns and the time involved in checking understandings and then opening the inquiry out for community knowledge to be shared. This way of 'being with' takes time and as Júlia commented earlier contrasts with the fast pedagogy of the worksheet. Next, permission to find different paths.

Going 'off track'

A slow pedagogy values the unexpected as Peter Moss emphasises here:

> It seemed to me that these are pedagogies that allow for and indeed value the unpredicted or the unexpected which allow for going in unexpected directions so they are not driven by the need to get somewhere which is already known but by an openness to exploring what is not known and which value things such as surprise. Again its Malaguzzi saying 'What has surprised you

today?' and it's also presumably a pedagogy which again recognises and values reflection, dialogue so basically time for thought and talk, time for discussion and isn't constrained . . . by the need to get somewhere by a certain time.

(Peter Moss, interview, May 2020)

Peter Moss continues by emphasising the open, exploratory nature of a slow pedagogy:

> You could say a *fast pedagogy is one where you know you have to get somewhere*, you know *what* the somewhere is and you know *when* you have to get there and there isn't any time to go off track. So slow pedagogy is about being open to exploration, to looking for somewhere new, those sort of metaphors like 'lines of flight', the idea of emergence . . . where people are saying 'let's see where this takes us'; 'That's really interesting, we need to understand that'; 'we need to go deeper into that' or 'I've never thought of that connection before', so it would be somewhere where people were digesting rather than just getting indigestion! Actually having time to work on things and think about things.

'Lines of flight' drawing on Deleuze and Guattari (2004) are the moments when something unexpected breaks the expected pattern of what comes next. Olsson explains: 'A line of flight runs like a zig-zag crack in between the other lines – and it is only these lines that, from the perspective of Deleuze and Guattari, are capable of creating something new' (Deleuze and Guattari 2004: 238 in Olsson 2009: 58). I like the idea of children finding a zig-zag crack or track that takes them into new ideas, new connections and relationships.

'Going off track' in a slow pedagogy can be seen as offering possibilities. This connects with the anthropologist Tim Ingold's concept of wayfaring (2015):

> In the carrying on of the wayfarer, every destination is by the way; his path runs always in between. The movement of the navigator, by contrast, are point-to-point, and every point has been arrived at, by calculation, even before setting off towards it.

(Ingold 2015: 133)

Solveig Nordtømme drew attention to the value of the in-between in our discussion:

> I love the concept 'in between'. So, I think that 'in between', could be one way of defining slow pedagogy because this is a small space for wondering, for a pause. . . . it's about thinking. In between is this magic space for possibilities and entanglements. Something can emerge without knowing how and to be prepared for it.
>
> So it's an alternative to this technical learning instrumental approach that 'if you use this, you will end up with this'. This is how I think about slow

pedagogy –it's not a way of doing it in a certain way but it's open, and it's ready for many possibilities.

(Solveig Nordtømme, interview, September 2020)

A wayfarer is unafraid of the unexpected and the unknown represents possibilities rather than distractions. Lynn McNair extends this idea of the wayfarer by describing the children themselves as 'wayfarers': (also see Hackett 2015):

It's in a similar way to Ingold's wayfaring, the child may have a destination, but they might take a different path to get there. Or they might have no destination really because they're moving and learning as they go along. And so we call the Cowgate children 'wayfarers' . . . children can take other roads on their developmental journey.

(Lynn McNair, interview, September 2020)

So the concept of a wayfarer can include acknowledgement and acceptance of difference rather than conformity. Gallacher explains this idea further in making the case for the adoption of Ingold's wayfaring metaphor in critiquing milestone metaphors in child development (Rose 1999): 'A key advantage of the wayfaring metaphor is that it allows for children to take other roads on their developmental journeys, and to follow their own (emergent rather than inbuilt) timetable' (Gallacher In Press).

Ingold (2015) contrasts

a 'crocodile' of children walking in file' and 'the caprice of the child-detective on the way to school: on arrival at the gates, the child – an *animal homificans* par excellence – submits to a regime intent on humanising its subjects through the imposition of adult discipline. Walking in a crocodile is no longer an open-ended practice of inquiry but a test to which the answers are given in advance.

(Ingold: 133)

Ingold's stark contrast between the unscripted walk to school and the tightly disciplined and scripted child in school raises a similar set of questions for young children in ECEC. A slow pedagogy may be seen to offer opportunities for wayfaring and curious 'child-detectives' to use Ingold's phrase, who have the opportunity to follow their interests and concerns. At the same time a less hurried approach can enable adults to stop and reflect on what are they curious about and on what they have learnt from and about the children they are with. This echoes Malaguzzi's question from earlier: 'What has surprised you today?'

Making time for children to go off track can also involve creating space for changing direction. This draws attention to the adults' role as the Danish early childhood adviser, Persille Schwartz explained:

Slow practices I regard as being present in the moment with the child/children and engaging in cocreation of what comes next – you carry your adult responsibility for the children being safe, but you support their exploration leaving your expectations and preunderstandings behind.

(Persille Schwartz, interview, September 2020)

Persille gave an example from an episode in a Danish kindergarten to illustrate how such *pedagogical improvisation* can develop. A necessarily detailed description follows to illustrate this point:

> In one place we were outside. And we've been doing a lot of standing on a hill fishing, . . . just imaginary things but we were fishing things out of a hole, and at some stage some other [children] wanted to join in, but they didn't want to fish . . . So we kind of moved away from there and we got to a place where there was a chestnut tree. And they've started to find these chestnuts. And one of the [children] was not finding one and getting upset about it. They got hold of these chestnuts, and then the pedagogue started talking about the chestnut and said 'Wow a chestnut! Did you know that it could be actually put in the ground and it could bloom and turn into this tree' . . . And then the child looked at her (and she's tapping into what is happening here) and there's just no reaction really. And the pedagogue looked at the boy and said: 'What is happening with your chestnut?' And then he looked at her and said: 'Well, my chestnut is broken but I'm sure my mom can fix it because she can sew everything' and it went into an exchange about the chestnut and how it could be repaired with rubber bands. The pedagogue followed that track instead of her original idea about 'you can put seeds in the ground'. This meandered into a conversation/exploration of how you might fix a broken chestnut: 'And you have a tiny little thing coming out of it . . . what then? What's next?' and then going down that track. Giving it the time to go in that direction instead of having a purpose. Being able to change track in the middle of it.
>
> *(Persille Schartz)*

In this account we see the pedagogue tuning in and catching the moment. She is firstly alert to the social and emotional landscape – being aware of which child is upset. Secondly, she starts a conversation about her knowledge about the natural properties of the chestnut but the child doesn't respond. So thirdly she asks a question: 'What about your chestnut?', which gives the stage to the child who takes the conversation in his own direction, bringing in knowledge about his mother's sewing skills and her ability to repair. The pedagogue's attentiveness is evident in this account. It isn't a letting go but a staying in the moment and remaining aware so the pedagogue is then ready to decide whether to follow or to make the next step. This seems to me to convey 'pedagogical improvisation', a phrase I first came across in conversation with Persille as we worked together on a Danish study: 'Professionals seeking children's perspectives' (Clark 2017: 135–141;

Eistrup 2016). Working with the Mosaic approach (see Chapter 10) as a starting point:

> Pedagogues chose which methods to apply and in what order, sometimes inventing methods, while remaining aware of the ethical underpinning of the study. This improvisation, following the children's lead, could take the research encounter in unplanned and unexpected directions, developing new 'dances' with children.
>
> *(Clark 2017: 137)*

Diving deep

A third related theme to emerge from my discussions about a slow pedagogy is the possibility of exploring in depth (Laevers 2000, 2015), children and adults 'diving deep' or 'digging deep' together. This is the antithesis of the 'depthlessness' that Stephen Ball cautions against (2010):

> Slow pedagogy . . . it's kind of the opposite of fast, hurry, it means to take time. And then in reading and thinking through its not just only concerning time. It's more about the deeper things. So at this moment, defining slow pedagogy is first of all about listening to and respecting every child's way of learning and living. Again, having dialogue with him or her, which means participating in the living word of the child. And to explore and go beyond the horizon of the existing world together, which means . . . solidarity.
>
> *(Mari Mori, interview, September 2020)*

Mari Mori's reflection, as an early childhood teacher educator in Japan, points to pedagogical relationships that are not shallow and on the surface but seek to create opportunities for deep inquiry, whether as adults, children or together. Across the discussion that follows you will see how the ability to go deeper was emphasised in different pedagogical contexts: in ECEC, in teacher education with students and in professional development.

Amanda Bateman's definition of a slow pedagogy, draws on her experience of early childhood teacher education and practice in Wales and New Zealand and on her research involving conversation analysis (Bateman 2015):

> Interactions between a teacher and child or children where talk and gesture explore and ponder a concept of interest *in great detail*. It is less about linear time. It doesn't have to be a *sustained* interaction, it's more about full engagement in the flow of *deep* time.
>
> *(Amanda Bateman, interview, September 2020)*

This draws attention to time for children and adults to use different modes of communication and a full immersion in the moment that is more concerned with the depth of the interaction rather than necessarily the length of the encounter. This emphasises for me the centrality of play with its 'full engagement in the flow of deep time'. There is the total absorption as seen in Tina Bruce's characteristics of play discussed in Chapter 3. These are not interactions governed by linear time but a deeper dimension.

The multimodal element of a slow pedagogy re-emerged in my discussion with Kate Cowan, who in turn introduced Jerome Bruner's concept of the spiral curriculum (Bruner 1960):

> So I found myself thinking about an idea of taking time to teach and learn deeply and meaningfully, and I was reminded of (I think it came up in my teacher training) of Bruner and the idea of the spiral curriculum . . . revisiting something at different levels And each time you revisit it you will revisit it slightly differently in slightly more depth. I think for me it's always kind of knotted up with this idea of recognising children's capacities in the widest sense. So, recognising that we make our signs of learning realised in multiple modes, it's not one or the other. And that children need time to be recognised and supported in education.
>
> *(Kate Cowan, interview, July 2020)*

There is an in-built temporal dimension to Bruner's concept of a spiral curriculum where repeated opportunities are given to revisit material. A slow pedagogy acknowledges that time is needed to go beyond a first glance and to enable multiple opportunities to revisit with close attention by educators to what new possibilities may emerge. We will discuss the question of revisiting further in Chapter 7 about slow practices and pedagogical documentation.

Biljana Fredriksen pointed to how a less fragmented timetable can create greater focus and depth, including in early childhood teacher education:

> Focusing on a few things rather than jumping from one to another, which has been the norm in curricular plans. There is so much you have to get through . . . in early childhood settings or in school or in university. There is a need to keep jumping within things too, checking that tasks are 'finished, finished, finished' and you don't really have time. You're not able to go in depth. So I believe it is more important to do a few things and to go in depth and then learn what learning in depth is and hopefully it will be possible to transfer that understanding of what learning in depth is to other subjects. So 'slow' means that you don't jump from one thing to another, and you don't rush, but you are more present, you have more room to be more attentive to what you're studying and also more attentive to how you're feeling and what you're sensing.
>
> *(Biljana Fredriksen, interview, October 2020)*

Biljana emphasises how time to focus is in short supply across every sector of education, in her experience. Multiple short-term, 'urgent' tasks distract from the ability to concentrate and explore in detail. She emphasises the importance for students studying to be early childhood educators to experience for themselves what exploring a topic in depth feels like, not in the abstract but as a synchronous activity, a live curriculum (see Chapter 6). The importance of firsthand, embodied experience that is attentive to feelings and the senses takes us back to Payne and Wattchow's account at the start of the chapter about a 'slow pedagogy of place' (2009).

The emphasis on deepening learning appeared once more in more conversation with Mara Krechevsky. In this extract Mara discusses insights gained from the long-standing research collaboration between the research centre, Project Zero at Harvard University and the preschools of Reggio Emilia.

ALISON: I was looking back on what you were saying earlier . . . and how it's so important how it's used, not just as I've heard said 'not just as wallpaper'. It is there for what comes out of it as much as the gathering.

MARA: Yes that's something that took me a long time to understand when collaborating with Reggio educators. Documentation is not just about making learning visible, and making learning visible is not an end in itself. I have colleagues who might disagree with me. This makes sense on one level, but I think the part of the definition that took us ten years to come up with that last phrase which is 'making learning visible *in order to deepen learning*'. You have something that you are interested in learning more about that can guide your documentation, because otherwise there's lots that you can document and make visible. How do you know what's most important to focus on? I think that relates to your purpose, whose learning is it that you want to deepen or support?

(Mara Krechevsky, interview, October 2020)

Mara emphasises here the importance of going beyond making learning visible through pedagogical documentation (see Chapter 7) in order to emphasise the primary purpose of deepening learning.

I would like to end this section by bringing us back to thinking with children:

And I think that, to be able to go in depth teachers really need to learn about that from the children because young children usually take the time they need before they're being rushed into moving on.

So, here we have to do the opposite. It's not the teachers teaching children to be slow, but the opposite. Teachers have to tune into the *children's* slow speed and then really appreciate play in sand or red leaves or whatever it is and try to go into that themselves. So, teachers slowing down or students slowing down is also about a genuine interest in what one can sense in the moment.

(Biljana Fredriksen, interview, October 2020)

So we have begun to explore the multi-faceted concept of a slow pedagogy and three of the emerging themes: 'Being with', going off track and diving deep. Here is a summary of some of the characteristics that will be expanded upon in the following chapters:

- A slow pedagogy is about 'being with' – attentive to the rhythm of the children, and adults and materials
- A slow pedagogy can involve rapid, intense moments as well as a slowing down of pace
- A slow pedagogy makes time for listening and collaboration
- A slow pedagogy celebrates the group as well as the individual
- A slow pedagogy values play and the present moment
- A slow pedagogy can take the long way, cultivating over time
- A slow pedagogy values the difficult to measure
- A slow pedagogy seeks to enable deep discovery and strengthen relationships

This leads us to the final part of this chapter to consider: what knowledge is valued if we are engaging with slow pedagogies in working with young children and with students? There is a close relationship between the process of teaching and learning and the forms of knowledge that such a way of working makes visible and values or ignores.

Slow knowledge

At the heart of this debate, I am challenging an epistemology – a view of knowledge that is concerned with facts; universal, easily packaged and delivered and measured. Instead, I am drawing attention to pedagogies that are in keeping with alternative views of knowledge in which complexity and interconnectedness are valued, where there is time for the unexpected and local knowledge is respected.

We can see this in the connection between the features of a slow pedagogy discussed in this chapter and the form of knowledge that may be brought to the surface and given status. Slow knowledge, for example, about a child's abilities and interests may take time to gather and require persistent listening to the child, siblings and parents and close attention to small details (see Chapter 10). Similarly, educators may gradually accumulate understandings about their role, as Deborah Harcourt explains:

> I would say that slow knowledge is understanding that is built over time. In contrast, I can build a body of knowledge that is very superficial. And I can know a lot about something, at that surface level. But what I'm trying to support educators to do is to 'deep dive' so that we're not doing breadth we're doing depth. So, giving yourself again the time to dig deeply into something, for example: 'How do I understand what to do and how to do it as an educator?' So that's what I would call slow knowledge, just forgetting

the breadth, picking the depth on a smaller number of topics, but at a much deeper, deeper level.

(Deborah Harcourt, interview, October 2020)

I ran a virtual reading group during this study, to think through ideas about the relationship with time in early childhood and slower ways of working. We began by discussing an article by the environmentalist David Orr (1996) on slow knowledge. He sets up a binary between fast knowledge and slow knowledge. Whilst I am aware that defining binaries can oversimplify, I have found the distinctions Orr describes as a helpful catalyst for thinking about what an epistemology that values 'slow' might look like. The list below is an extract from Orr's description of fast and slow knowledge.

- Fast knowledge deals with discrete things; *slow knowledge deals with context, patterns, and connections . . .*
- Fast knowledge is mostly linear; *slow knowledge is complex and ecological . . .*
- Fast knowledge is characterised by power and instability; *slow knowledge is known by its elegance, complexity, and resilience . . .*
- Fast knowledge is often abstract and theoretical, engaging only a portion of the mind. *Slow knowledge engages all of the senses and the full range of our mental powers.*
- Fast knowledge is always new; *slow knowledge often is very old.*

(Emphasis added. Extracts from Orr 1996: 699–702)

Drawing on Orr's definition, slow knowledge deals with context and therefore gives status to local and indigenous knowledge. It has time to recognise patterns and connections between ideas, shared conversations and events. These patterns might stretch over days, weeks or years as educators pay close attention to children's views, experiences and discoveries, perhaps involving peers, older siblings and families. Slow knowledge may not necessarily follow in a straight line and can be difficult to measure or duplicate. This is knowledge that can be durable or, as Orr comments, has 'resilience'. Slow knowledge may be 'old'. This suggests that a learning community that values slow knowledge is not afraid to draw on traditions. Sometimes new ideas will emerge but there is not a need for 'always new'. It may involve being more open to reclaim old knowledge.

In the chapters that follow I hope to show some of the practices that can enable these forms of slow knowledge to develop in ECEC, that are unafraid of complexity, are deep-rooted and can draw on long traditions. Such knowledge may be expressed by young children and adults about lived experience in myriad different ways, and in so doing challenge what is taken for granted or remains hidden.

Conclusion

This chapter has set out to begin to make explicit the possible ingredients of a slow pedagogy. The definitions shared have been constructed out of dialogue and are markers in an ongoing process as more educators make explicit how they relate to time in ECEC and describe the slow practices they have developed.

We now turn to exploring what slow practices look like in ECEC in the following six chapters. This will be an opportunity to consider in more detail: what does a slow pedagogy look like, and what forms of knowledge can be created and made visible? What kind of environments support these alternative relationships with time? What can we understand further about the role of educators in a less hurried approach, and what political and practical issues may arise? This is the starting point for Part 2.

Questions

1   What would you see as the key ingredients of a slow pedagogy?
2   What opportunities do young children have to 'go off track' to follow their own ideas and interests in ECEC?
3   What do you see as the key attributes of educators if children are seen as 'wayfarers'?

PART 2

Slow pedagogies and slow practices

What does slow look like in early childhood education?

Introduction

Time is a slippery subject. Once you start to reflect on what time is and how we relate to it then what might have been a straightforward, taken-for-granted concept becomes far more complex (Murris and Kohan 2021). Reconsidering multiple understandings of time can be uncomfortable work, particularly if this thinking is taking place within the context of institutions that are governed by the clock. I am drawing on different examples of practice in these chapters from early childhood education and beyond to help find ways to see what is currently happening and draw attention to alternatives.

Part 2 provides demonstrations and discussion of what attention to time can look like in ECEC. I set out to explore what are the slow practices and in what contexts are they happening? This is the opportunity to look in more detail at what working with slow pedagogies and constructing slow knowledge in practice and research with young children might look like.

Chapter Five begins with exploring slow practices in place, both outdoors and indoors, followed in Chapter Six by a focus on slow practices with materials including in the specific environment of the studio. Chapter Seven looks in some detail at the process of pedagogical documentation through a temporal lens. The discussion then turns to slow practices in everyday routines in Chapter Eight, followed by looking at slow practices and stories in Chapter Nine. The relationship between slow practices in research and listening is explored in Chapter Ten to conclude Part 2. Throughout these chapters examples are discussed about working with slow practices in early childhood teacher education.

The slow practices I have chosen to discuss are not intended as a definitive list but as a catalyst for reflection. The practices are divided into chapters to fit

DOI: 10.4324/9781003051626-6

the format of a book or series of lectures. However, the ideas discussed relate to each other and there are blurred boundaries between each of them, for example between slow practices in place, with materials and in the everyday. I invite you to make your own tracks through the pages that follow . . .

5

SLOW PRACTICES IN PLACE

Introduction

What is it about being outdoors that can invite a different relationship with time?

One of the catalysts for thinking about slow pedagogies grew through my conversations with Kari-Anne Jørgensen-Vitterso, one of my Norwegian colleagues. Kari-Anne, as an ECEC teacher educator and researcher, has written widely about young children's engagement over time with the natural environment (for example Jørgensen 2016; Beery and Jørgensen 2018). Kari-Anne invited me to join one of her teaching sessions with international early childhood master's students on a visit to a forest kindergarten in a wooded coastal area by the Oslo Fjord, in South-Eastern Norway. Having spent time with the young children in the woods observing their play, the students were then engaged in working on activities with natural materials. I have two vivid memories of the day. In the morning I remember young children playing in small groups among the trees and two adults sitting on the ground nearby. The atmosphere felt relaxed and at the same time purposeful as the young children moved logs, arranged their dens and chatted together. The second memory is from the afternoon of activities with the university students involving building a rope ladder. As I listened to Kari-Anne discuss with students what they had learnt during the day, I drew with a piece of burnt wood on the wet rock. My physical engagement with the materials around seemed to anchor the memory of the day.

Talking with Kari-Anne, I asked, 'what would pedagogy look like if what I was seeing outdoors came indoors?' It was in one sense a feeling, the essence of an experience, rather than an easily measured difference between the relationships and encounters that were happening outdoors in contrast to indoors. This question centred around bringing the outside in – not literally, but in terms of pedagogy – and in particular the attitudes and values contained therein.

DOI: 10.4324/9781003051626-7

This chapter starts by looking in more detail at the opportunities for engaging in slow practices with young children outdoors, before moving indoors to consider some aspects of the links between the spatial and temporal in a classroom. The chapter ends by removing the walls altogether.

We start with a walk through a forest to the Beaver Dam.

Relationships with place unfolding over time

I discussed in Chapter 4 how the concept of a 'slow pedagogy of place' (Payne and Wattchow 2009) has grown out of environmental education, concerns about 'take-away' tick sheet pedagogies and a desire to promote sustainability. Drawing primarily on examples from my interviews I explore the effect of a slow and repeated relationship for young children with outdoor spaces over time. The first example is a reflection by Karin Andrews Jashapara, who leads Forest school sessions in a Steiner-influenced school with six-year-olds.

The Beaver Dam

So there's a place in the woodland that one group calls the Beaver Dam. Our site is flanked by two rivers, one bigger, the other more like a big stream. The children are allowed near the smaller one. There are lots of logs in it, and in working on their Beaver Dam they enjoy throwing more logs in or taking them out or scrambling them. The water carries the weight of these big objects, so the children are able to move them around by prodding them with the long poles they find. The river is a huge magnet in their 'self-directed learning', their free play. They watch the dam, listening with delight to the changing noises of its changing shapes – a cry will go up 'we've made a whirlpool!' or on returning another week, running to see it, 'it's become a waterfall, come and hear the sounds!'

They had a story in the classroom last year about a beaver, which they loved. And so that was the thought it started with, they want to help beavers, real or imagined.

By the stream there's a rise on the bank, overhung with lots of trees and vines which form a sort of cave. They climb up into this shelter and they have this teamwork . . . running energetically up and down the river, now and then finding a huge log to work with. I feel honoured when they ask me to join them, but I tend to stand back. They do great teamwork with big logs or fallen branches, which they've learned to carry safely. And they also know about disturbing habitat; we think we probably won't, as long as we check first, especially by looking for minibeasts in damp wood. They are creating new habitats, by shifting the wood around.

(Karin Andrews Jashapara, interview, September 2020)

This account brings to life the interconnection between the imaginary and the material world that has been able to develop in this place that has become familiar to the children. Karin indicates the practical skills and confidence that has flourished under her supervision. Both the physical and social can come together. Karin continues:

> They do lots of role play, so for example I saw a very shy and gentle boy standing like a sentinel and demanding a 'fee' from anyone who wanted to get past him. The students practise crossing an improvised, strong but wobbly, log bridge that others leave. It is a matter of balancing, and using a stick if necessary for stability. Mostly they take pride in crossing unassisted. It is good 'risk tolerance', in Forest School terms. An adult is nearby. One boy, who is boldly imaginative but can be a little timid, was working up the courage to cross over. I asked, 'Are you sure you're alright to cross over?' I've been very guarded about letting them cross the river generally but I know this is not too risky and rather a good challenge. And he said immediately, 'If I don't try I won't get anywhere'. It brings that out of them, I think, courage, and independence, with deeper understanding of risk, and how to build their own confidence.
>
> *(Karin Andrews Jashapara)*

When discussing with my study participants where might they have encountered slow practices with young children from their own experience, several drew attention to the unfolding of relationships with place, outdoors. Kate Cowan, recollecting her teaching experience commented:

> In terms of practice, so one of the things . . . I did that really felt slow and in a good way . . . really rich was when I was teaching we worked with an organisation called Cambridge Curiosity and Imagination, who were a group of artists in Cambridge, and they take inspiration from Reggio inspired approaches as well and we did a project with them that we called our Footprints project. So we went to a local area of woodland for eight weeks at a time, once a week, and took all of the children, and spent the whole morning there . . . .We went with the values of listening to children and following their fascinations, so it really started out very slow. Lots of listening, lots of looking, watching, observing, discussing reflecting and, then over those weeks noticing children's fascinations and we ended up writing a little book of children's stories that they told in the wood.
>
> *(Kate Cowan, interview, July 2020)*

I am interested in the qualities that the educators brought to these repeated encounters: 'listening, looking, watching, discussing, reflecting' and later documenting. Waller (2006) discusses a similar benefit for young children of revisiting of a familiar environment over time and the depth of imaginative play that can develop. The listening led to a heightened awareness of what the children were drawn to and fascinated by (see Chapter 7). Kate continues:

> and that was where some of my interest around children's movement really came in because there was a comment from, I think, one of the teachers who

said: 'Well those children are just running, the other ones are doing productive focused stuff and they're just running around, we need to bring them
back'. I've always thought 'are we a bit too quick to dismiss physical play as
something that's not as worthwhile as other forms of investigation?' The children were focused, they were focused on running and weaving through and
getting lost and playing tricks with perspective. But it took us time to work
that out. And we did that through giving the children video cameras to take
with them while they ran and giving them opportunities to draw maps to
show us where they had been and things like that so we tried to treat it with
respect and as something important. It was through that kind of slow looking
and listening and really trying to unpick something that was challenging to us
as educators, and not dismissing it. This was a real interesting line of inquiry
and something that has stuck with me.

(Kate Cowan)

This description brings me back to Kate's thoughts on slow pedagogy, discussed
in Chapter 4: 'I think it's seeing learning as something that you do with children
rather than to children, and something that has time for wonder and uncertainty.'
Learning here is together with children, where listening is key and educators are
not afraid of both uncertainty and complexity.

Timefullness – time to talk

Continuing with outdoors environments, I am interested in how slow practices
outdoors may enable 'timefullness' (Chapter 4) where there is an opening up or
expansive view of time. Amanda Bateman, in her interview, drew attention to
research with Jane Waters (Waters and Bateman 2015) involving the temporal affordances of outdoor spaces for young children and educators:

The outdoor space seems to provoke a lot more of this rich contextual
unpacking of things. This concept exploration and working at a really good
pace . . .. Jane did notice that children initiate questions and interactions
more in outdoor areas than they do inside but also I was interested in the way
that the teachers are responding as they seem to have much more time. And
they seem calmer with their responses and really explore whatever it is that
the child is interested in much more fully than when they're indoors. I'm not
quite sure why that is. I think maybe the change in the context, perhaps . . .
but I wonder if it's because you feel like you're already doing your job so you
don't need to justify yourself because you are already out going on the walk.

You don't need to justify yourself by thinking 'what am I doing now with
a child?' because you're outdoors and you're doing this walking and the child
has come to you and asked you so you can actually just talk to them about
things.

(Amanda Bateman, interview, September, 2020)

Tahmina Shayan succinctly summarised the different relationship with time that is possible in the early childhood centre where she is involved:

> The centre is nature focused and we are outside most of the day. I can see that we have no clock outside and that having no clock invites a slower pedagogy because we are not facing the clock but children.

I am left with a strong sense across the interviews of the different relationship with time being linked to a release outdoors from internal pressure to perform. This was echoed by educators in the focus group:

> I feel like for me, it happens quite naturally when I'm outside with children. So inside . . . I don't know whether it's the ringing bells or the timetables or the scheduling but I feel much more like I have a specific role when I'm in a classroom where as soon as I'm outside that role shifts, and I'm just there with the children. We went to the woods once a week. And just that sort of regular connection to a place. We packed our bags and we had everything we needed for the day. There wasn't going to be any systems or bells and we had our food, we had everything we needed and we were just ready to respond. I definitely feel like being outside allows that to happen much more naturally than when I'm in the classroom at our school'.
>
> *(Grace Haines, focus group, April 2021)*

Grace's comments give an insight into the shift in roles that she feels from working with young children in the classroom to their weekly trip to the woods. There is a sense here of being able to give oneself permission to relate differently to children and to perhaps perform less (see Chapter 2). Katie McCracken, another member of the focus group continues:

> I work in a setting that's outdoors all the time, we're fully outdoors all year. The children definitely seem like they belong to the setting. When they arrive the children convey a confidence as if they are saying 'I'm in control here and I can do what I want with the environment, that's around me'. It's funny because we've got a small indoor space where they come back to have dinner, and they get ready for the day there. But there's that kind of small space in between the time that they go and join the others to be outside for the day where we tend to think they have to be doing something inside whether that's drawing or puzzles and more indoor things. Whereas the outdoor space (although we obviously set up ladders and swings and they've got the tree to climb and things), there's the space where they can just go and do what they want, they can make up their own play.
>
> *(Katie McCracken, focus group, April 2021)*

These brief accounts have drawn attention to the interconnections between the spatial and temporal in respect to early childhood practices outdoors and raised the question of a freedom from the need to perform, or perhaps, to refer to Rosa, less of a need to 'run ever faster' (2019: 415; see Chapter 1).

Rooms, relationships and slow practices

The focus of this chapter on slow practices and place now moves indoors. Here the intention is to consider how time might be entangled with practices, relationships and design that each influence everyday life in ECEC for children and educators. This builds on my discussion in Chapter 2 about 'Clocktime'. This reminds me of an earlier research study I took part in involving the design and practices associated with three post-war primary schools designed by Mary (Crawley) Medd and David Medd (Burke 2013; Clark 2010b). This was a period of post-war school design in England where architectural intent and educational philosophy worked closely together with attention to the liveability of the space.

I was fortunate to meet Judy, a welfare assistant or welfare helper as she was known, during a visit to one of the case studies, an Infant school (for children between four and seven years old). This led to a microstudy of the 'welfare room' that had been Judy's base for 16 years of the more than 30 years she had worked in the school (Clark, 2010b). An analysis of the role of the welfare helper, the objects and the practices that took place in the room pointed to the living out of two different but related discourses: a discourse of comfort and care and a discourse of craft.

The room contained a bed, with a blanket and Winnie the Pooh pillowcase and a chair. Judy described how children were able to choose a cuddly toy and sometimes a hot water bottle, signifying comfort. The chair was also important:

> Children might sit there whilst having a scraped knee mopped up but the chair signified a particular relationship with an adult within the school: 'Children could sit in the chair and chat'. The chair represented a place for conversations, which suggests an unhurried environment where there was time for children to sit and be listened to. This links to the function of the room as a listening space for emotional support as well as physical illness:
>
> Sick children came to us in the room if they were ill. The Head would say 'Do you think she should go home?' If the children had a problem at home or stomachache the teacher might bring them along – if they thought they needed a little 'TLC' [tender loving care] and they would tell you because if they did have something that was worrying them they would be more likely to tell one of us.

(Clark 2010b: 773)

I am interested, in rereading this account, how the chair supported an '*unhurried environment* where there was *time for children to sit and be listened to.*' The slow practices of listening and care are entangled with the furniture and design of the room as a 'non–classroom' in between space. The welfare room was also associated with the preparation of teaching materials:

> It was a place for 'making' and a place of apprenticeship. This was an environment where routine tasks were undertaken but with a pride in the time and care taken and attention to detail: 'You had your jobs to do but you had more time. You could do everything in there.'
>
> *(Clark 2010b: 774)*

One of the tasks performed involved preparing the displays of children's work. Children who came to the welfare room, and were well enough, were encouraged to help in the preparing of materials and were encouraged to extend their creative skills. It seems that the relationships Judy established with the children appeared to embody an expansive relationship with time or timefullness in order for craft and care to take place. The welfare room was a liminal space that existed outside some of the restrictions of timetabled life in the school; it held time and the present moment in a particular way (see Dyer 2018a).

Next, I focus on time practices within a classroom rather than an 'in-between' space.

This example looks at how introducing a new designed feature within a classroom may or may not present opportunities for a different sense of time, based on a design intervention by Emma Dyer, who was one of my research participants. Emma's doctoral study combined the disciplines of architecture and education (Dyer 2018b). Her study, based in an English primary school with five- and six-year-olds, explored the places to read provided for beginner readers. A focus on *where* children could read and the impact on design led to Emma creating a child-sized, semi-enclosed 'Reading Nook'. Following Emma's doctoral research she arranged to trial introducing the reading nooks into two Primary Year One classrooms, with five- and six-year-old children in England. The teaching approach and ethos of the classroom had a profound impact on how children related to and worked with the new structure. In the first school:

> Everything was extremely heavily timetabled. And there was that real sense of 'we've got to do our reading now, we've got to do our writing now' . . . it was just on, on, on. The children were very, very, occupied all the time. So [the teacher] only allowed them to go inside the nook and look when they were doing something called 'Guided reading'. So there would be a group of six children who would be allowed to go inside . . . that was a point when they were allowed to read independently. So, in terms of slow pedagogy, the rest of the class we're all doing tasks, and this one group of children were allowed to just explore books. And they really had fun and played with it . . . . They were interesting with time actually. They got hold of a timer, and they were timing each other to make sure that certain children weren't allowed too long in it. So, they were policing it. But they were reading to

each other. And they were just exploring different books and they obviously weren't sitting at their desks. And one of the features of the design was that there needed to be enough room for them to lie down. They would sprawl across the floor and it was a very different sort of space, and it was really interesting to watch that, while the rest of the class was doing focused activities, and sometimes the teacher would say that they were being too noisy, because once they were inside they lost all awareness of their being in class. She'd say 'Stop [being] so noisy!'

(Emma Dyer, interview, June 2020)

There is a strong sense from this account of how the impact of the 'Reading Nook' in this first classroom was heavily influenced by the ethos within the room. The structure did serve in some ways to disrupt the relationship with time experienced by the children in this classroom. However, what is interesting to note is how the children adopted the role of 'time managers', taking over control of the sand timer in order to 'police' how long their peers had access to the reading space.

An identical structure had a very different affect when introduced in a different school to a class of children who were also five and six years old. Here is Emma's reflection on the teacher's response to the Reading Nook in this second school:

She was the most amazing teacher I think I've ever seen . . .. she had the most difficult class of, I think, about 34 or 35 children; it wasn't a big classroom. She totally inhabited this idea of the Nook coming in. She didn't tell the children beforehand. She told them that it had arrived, and she didn't know what it was or what to use it for, and she invited them all to speculate and paint and draw it. And then they all decorated it . . .. And she incorporated it into so many aspects per lesson, and . . . the children really took it over in a very different way. And they would do a lot of singing and they would talk in a different way when they were inside, so they weren't really reading as much they would be doing songs, it was a very imaginative space . . .. it really had a different sense of time and space compared to what was happening outside in the classroom.

So I mean both of them did, but that one it was like a sort of Time Machine . . .. It was such a different space. And a lot of that was down to the teacher, and her relaxation of the space, she kind of let go of that and let them have that . . .. When you're observing or researching whatever in classrooms I think you don't often see the teacher letting children have control over a space. So, I think using the word 'slower' not to necessarily mean just not doing anything but changing the time. That was a really interesting thing to watch . . . quite unique.

(Emma Dyer)

So what ideas does this example raise about slow practices and place? Emma describes the structure she introduced into the two classrooms as a 'time machine'– it had an effect. The teacher in the first school who struggled with the design intervention is a reminder of how the introduction of change that 'disrupts' both the spatial and temporal relationships in a classroom can be disconcerting and challenging. Introducing a resource will not necessarily change the relationship with time within a learning space. The influence of the designed change was closely linked to the teaching ethos and to patterns of relating to time that the children had embodied. The participatory pedagogy evident in the second classroom where the children were invited to play an active, exploratory role, opened up more possibilities for creating different relationships with time, in keeping with Wein's observation:

> Oddly the only way I know to break the dominance of time organisation is to focus attention on the organisation of space, to make changes to the environment and to watch children's responses, and in the process to '*let time go*'.
> *(Wien 1995: 136 quoted in Wien and Kirby-Smith 1998)*

School Without Walls – a different relationship with time?

The final example of slow practices and place blurs the boundaries between indoors and outdoors. The School Without Walls project (Hay 2018) puts arts education at the centre of learning and takes learning out of the confines of the physical educational institution. The project originated in 2010 as a collaboration between Penny Hay, Director of research at the arts organisation 5 x 5 x5 + creativity, Sue East the Head teacher of St Andrews Primary School in Bath and the Director of the egg Theatre Bath. The project deconstructs the curriculum and breaks away from a rigid subject-led timetable in primary school. This whole school approach has given children the opportunity to participate in 'residencies' of five weeks with the local theatre called 'the egg' and shorter mini-residencies. One of the educators involved, Graeme describes the pedagogical approach as 'an activist-style, hands-on, dive-in kinaesthetic learning'[1]). He describes the different relationship with time that occurs, linking this to Csikszentmihalyi's concept of flow (1990, 1997): 'The ego flies away. Time flies . . .. Maybe our experience of time whizzes by at the 'egg' is a sign that we are in the zone.'

So in this example leaving the walls of school behind has opened up a different relationship with time in several ways. Firstly, the suspension of the timetable for the days that the children are in residence in the theatre establishes a new relationship with time that isn't constrained by subject boundaries. Secondly, there seems to be the opportunity for immersion in the creative activities taking place that as Graeme explains changes the rhythm and pace, making it seem that 'time flies'. Bath, the city in which the school is situated, is seen as an open resource to be connected to in increasingly diverse ways.

Penny Hay explains the importance of the principles on which the initiative is based: 'The underlying belief, influenced by Fondazione Reggio Children Foundation, is that if children are invited to follow their fascinations, as artists and creative explorers, their motivation and interests explode.'

It is interesting to reflect on how many of these principles demonstrate timefull-ness and call for unfragmented time:

School Without Walls Creative Manifesto

1 Be free to follow your fascinations
2 Ask and explore your own questions
3 Trust in your own ideas and interests
4 Express yourself
5 Work independently
6 Create a safe space to take risks
7 Attempt without the fear of failure
8 Be ok with the unknown
9 Be kind
10 Remember all our ideas matter
11 Choose how you do things
12 Be creative!
13 Do things in a different way
14 Cherish everyone's individual way of doing things
15 Think outside the bubble
16 Use your senses
17 Create time and space to explore and learn
18 Make real life choices
19 Be happy, engaged and achieve your best
20 Feel connected to your city and community

(www.creativityexchange.org.uk/ideas-hub/school-without-walls)

Discussion

Holding the present moment: outdoors and indoors

It was noticeable how many of the study participants drew attention to slow prac-tices unfolding over time in outdoor environments. Some of the places discussed were natural uncultivated spaces, such as the forest described by Karin Andrews Jashapara. However other spaces took the form of a traditional 'school' playground with a tarmacked surface. An overriding consideration seemed to be: how was play enabled to flourish in such spaces?

Looking at these environments through a temporal lens draws attention to how access to a natural environment, over time, can in some ways break the hold of the clock and the timetable.

Such spaces can offer the opportunity for 'nonfragmented time' that Cuffaro identified (see Chapter 4). What perhaps we see in the examples discussed is the opportunities offered to young children in both unfragmented time and repeated visits to enable an accumulation of place and play knowledge. This however cannot be looked at in isolation to the relationships and interactions between children and adults.

Disrupting the time/table

But does drawing attention to the slow practices that can happen outdoors and the creation of a relationship with time that is unfragmented and rooted in place have any bearing on how young children spend their time in indoor ECEC environments? The example of Emma's 'Reading Nook' raises the question of how changes to a designed element of the classroom may disrupt the relationship with time. The introduction of a new space within the classroom can affect established patterns and enable different practices to happen, in this case involving children's engagement with reading. However, the impact of the design intervention is dependent on how pedagogy is understood in the learning institution within which it sits and in educators' responses to what is of value, supported or disallowed.

Drawing on Emma's description of the Reading Nook as a 'time machine', such a device might enable children to experience time in a different way than the linear, clock-driven sense of time. Some of the accounts in this chapter indicate how having access to familiar outdoor natural environments may act as 'time machines' for both children and educators, with opportunities to establish a different relationship with time.

Another form of disrupting the 'time/table' may be to collaborate with other organisations that support a less structured and less scripted approach, as we saw in the 'School Without Walls' example. MacRae et al. (2021) identify the possibilities of such engagement over time between young children, their families and museums:

> Threading through the temporal qualities at play during and across visits, key themes come to the fore: the unpredictability of how encounters with the museum unfold: the comfort and the joy of the anticipation of the familiar and the emergence of ritual, and finally the pleasure of losing oneself in time.
> *(MacRae et al. 2021: 136)*

There seems a parallel here between the enjoyment of repeated visits to familiar environments seen earlier in the outdoor examples together with the additional joy in the unexpected. MacRae, Hackett and Holmes identify the flow between the familiar and the unfamiliar and the importance of both sets of experiences for young children:

> This temporal back and forth, between the familiar and the unfamiliar gives rise to the emergence of rhythms that connect with place; places in (and out) of the museum that feel both safe and unsafe. Familiar spaces and objects invite an engagement that is obvious and predictable, while unfamiliar places

and strange things have the potential to set in motion wonder, 'exploring' and ambiguous feelings. This is a constant and oscillating movement between the known and the not yet known.

(*MacRae et al. 2021: 142*)

Conclusion

This chapter has pieced together examples of slow practices in a range of different environments in order to probe what makes a less hurried relationship with time possible in these places. We have encountered how 'timefullness' may be experienced through repeated visits to a familiar outdoor environment, theatre space or museum. Such extended moments may take place in less visible places, where young children receive care and are deeply listened to.

We turn next to how the specific environment of a studio may create further opportunities for disrupting the clock.

Questions

1   What do you see as the possible value of children becoming familiar with the same outdoor environment over repeated visits?
2   Why might being in natural outdoor environments support less hurried ways of engaging with young children?
3   What activities might act as a 'time machine' within ECEC enabling children to experience time in a different way?

Note

1   www.creativityexchange.org.uk/ideas-hub/school-without-walls

6

SLOW PRACTICES AND MATERIALS

Introduction

This chapter discusses how materials can hold time in different ways ((Lemke 2000). It is a brief exploration of how viewing the arts as a way of knowing relates to rethinking the relationship with time in ECEC. Building on Chapter 5 about slow practices and place, we visit the studio as a generator of slow knowledge. This is a dedicated environment where an emphasis on the relationships between materials, the space and young children can open up a different temporal dimension for both children and adults. The studio is a place for thinking, where new possibilities emerge from listening and lingering (Kind et al. 2019). Questions will be raised about the role of early childhood educators and teacher education if knowledge construction or co-construction is viewed in this way.

I come to this chapter as both an academic and a visual artist. My own approach to ways of knowing has developed through teaching, writing, research with young children and making (Clark 2012). My arts practice involves engaging with a range of materials including ink, pastels, charcoal and paint together with the natural environment. The relationship with *time* has become an explicit feature of my art, through for example the slow practice of sewing (Wellesley-Smith 2015). Being a maker has informed my 'personal pedagogy' (Van Manen 2016: 11) and as a result I have chosen to include in this chapter more dialogue between myself and my participants. It is also an indication of how exchange has been at the centre of this study. My intention has not been to extract information but in keeping with the pedagogical approaches explored, to co-construct understandings about the processes involved in slow pedagogies and slow knowledge together. Central to these discussions have been colleagues from an arts education background, as Biljana Fredriksen explains:

DOI: 10.4324/9781003051626-8

> When you deal with the Arts then I guess the 'slowliness' of pedagogy has always been there because the creative process demands that you are present and you're making your own choices, and that takes time.
>
> *(Biljana Fredriksen, interview, October 2020)*

We start with a ball of clay.

Clay: different relationships with time

Clay found its way into several conversations with participants about slow practices and materials. I begin with a description of working with 'clay time' by Sylvia Kind who is an instructor and researcher based in a studio:

> We're working with clay and my students think I am a bit strange until they get into it. What does it mean to think about 'clay time'? The time of clay is slow. It is formed slowly through slow moving rivers over hundreds of years. And so what does it mean to work with clay?
>
> And what if you are studying trees? What is 'tree time?' That's a different kind of time, those are slow times . . . so we participate with the times of the things we are studying. You know that you can really slow to clay time . . . so we do things like bring the clay to the river to work with it there. So the clay goes back to where it came from and to see it melt into the water and to find its way again and you begin to participate with it. This is why I love Tim Ingold's writing, particularly where he writes about correspondences, about participating with materials. This idea of corresponding with materials. And I guess that for me is such an important aspect, whether you are working with children or with adult students or educators, is this idea of not just using a material or an idea to do something with it. But how do we participate with it, to move with it, to correspond with it which then has huge implications in terms of how we create spaces.
>
> *(Sylvia Kind, interview, November 2020)*

Thinking about 'participating with materials' introduces theoretical perspectives from posthumanism that place an active role on the environment and materials (Lenz Taguchi 2010; Moss 2019: 141–169), that can be understood as an intra-active pedagogy:

> intra-action is about something happening 'in-between different bodies'. The concept of 'in-between' is important for rethinking agency, moving from a simple idea of A acting upon B to a more complex idea of entanglements out of which intra-action emerges something new.
>
> *(Moss 2019: 147)*

We continue with clay in this extract from my discussion with Kari Carlsen, artist and early childhood teacher educator who has engaged over many years with the ideas and practices in the pre-schools in Reggio Emilia (Carlsen 2015, 2021):

ALISON: Do you want to just give me an example of a material that 'holds' time, that has 'long ways of transformation'?

KARI: I have had the experience of clay that can lead to extended ways of exploring because you can get the clay from the soil. You find the place where the earth is more or less made of clay. And then you dig it up, and it holds more or less material from around it. It could be sand, of course, but also small pieces of earth and leaves and so on. It can have different qualities. And you can give children time to explore these different qualities when you dig it up. There's a lot of learning and exploring the different phases of clay. And then it's a question of what do you do with this clay? It depends on the age of the children, the smallest ones will pull it into small pieces. Then there are many different ways of exploring clay. What happens when you add sand to clay? What does the clay do, if we connect it to a trunk of a tree outdoors? What is happening when we take the clay inside, or if it is still outside when it rains or when it's sunny? Is it possible to thin it out with water? Paint with it? It has unlimited ways of transformation. And then there is the drying process in different environments and then the firing processes. There is a shift from the dark grey malleable substance to the dry material that has cracks. And what if you put it in a fire? Many Norwegian kindergartens have a fire pan, to make the fire in a safe way and then put the clay things into it and look at the transformation. And then the children experience the clay really glowing red when it comes to 500 or 600 degrees in the fire. And then it is really hot. You have to stand a bit away. And then when it's cooler you can feel that it's not really cold, but it will be cold. You can work with all your senses and then ceramics are one of the most stable materials that we know, as archaeology tells us. So it's possible to connect all these phases of clay to cultural moments too. Clay presents a really big picture starting with small moments, through the history of the material that you can tell children about.

The fallen tree

Here is another example of how young children can be given the opportunity to experience materials that hold time in particular ways. The architect Pallasmaa refers to how a natural object can retain a memory of its past:

> A pebble polished by waves is pleasurable to the hand, not only because of its soothing shape but because it expresses the slow process of its formation; a perfect pebble on the palm materialises duration, it is time turned to shape.
>
> *(2012: 56–58)*

Kari Carlsen describes here the opportunities presented to young children and early childhood students by a fallen tree.

> A tree. Sometimes, also in towns, trees have to be cut down. Here in the countryside. that's not a problem. There are always owners who are cutting down trees. And to bring a big tree into the kindergarten and start with 'Oh here is a big tree, with its crown and all the branches.'
>
> And they start using their bodies by hanging, jumping, walking, balancing, and so on. And then it's possible to take the parts: What colour are the leaves? What's happening when they dry? During this process I'm thinking: 'What sort of things are possible to play with here? Thin elements and thicker parts of the tree?' You can use a saw together. I always use this big saw that has two handles so you can saw back and forth with the children and cut the tree up into small pieces or with an axe. You can have small pieces or bigger pieces that could be built into patterns with different colours. Then you have the bark. It is possible to take bigger or smaller pieces of bark. And then you have the wood. What could we do with the wood? What's happening when it's drying? And then the children can use a knife, of course, and the adults, to see how can we make marks in this branch? . . .
>
> So you see there are a lot of different ways of using a tree instead of getting these pieces readymade. It's the long, long ways of transformation. I think that's one of the main things I teach my students.
>
> *(Kari Carlsen, interview, September 2020)*

Clay and the fallen tree are holding time in a particular way but if we apply the idea of an intra-activity pedagogy these explorations can be understood as an entanglement between branches, clay, adults, children, weather and time. Merewether (2019) refers to the term 'murmurations', as seen in the swirling movement of a flock of birds in flight, to express the dynamic nature of such entanglements between the human and nonhuman.

We turn next to thinking in more detail about transformations in an early childhood studio.

Studio: a generator of slow knowledge

We start here with the atelierista Vea Veechi's account of practices in the studio in the Diana school in Reggio Emilia, Italy (Vecchi 2010), through the lens of slow pedagogy and the relationship with time.

Veechi reflects on the relationship with time in education:

> Today, more than ever, attention to the project is important because haste seems to have become urgently important for younger generations; when projects exist they are often short-lived and rapidly replaced by ones of even shorter duration. Interests on the other hand are multitudinous, almost

greedily so, and have the brief lifetime of an emotion, of a gesture; to the extent that 'acts are very often consumed in the gesture'.

(Galimberti 2008: 278; Vecchi 2010: 38)

Veechi emphasises the role of the learning context, the atelier, in the process of enabling techniques to become languages:

I have often recounted, to the point of almost reducing my opinion to a slogan, how ateliers can and must make techniques *become languages*, how the ability to execute a technique must be developed in the context of broader and more complex meaning.

(Vecchi 2010: 38)

This 'becoming' is by necessity time-consuming as is the painstaking process of acquiring a new language. Creating new expressive vocabulary in this way can be understood as a form of slow knowledge. Veechi identifies another feature involved here that relates to time – the ability to wait for children to discover both problems and possible solutions:

Malaguzzi used to say that the work of a teacher is for 'professional marvellers'. The definition is truly beautiful; a message of hope for such a delicate profession. If we are not capable of waiting for the awareness that what children's research generates will probably surprise us and also surprise them, then our job will almost certainly be less interesting and less fun, the climate of learning different and probably less productive for both children and teacher.

(Vecchi 2010: 47)

This attentive waiting is a form of listening: 'Working in a playful, unscripted way with materials may enable listening to happen 'differently' and for slow knowledge to develop' (Clark 2020: 142). A studio is a place of making, of craft. Tim Ingold, the anthropologist whose work Sylvia Kind referred to earlier, discusses the different temporal speeds that can be at play here: 'The skill, the trick of the craftsman is one who can hold the forward moving momentum of the imagination with the slow movement of holding with materials' (Ingold, lecture 2012). This holding of fast, forward momentum and slow together seems to fit well with what can happen in a studio with children and with adults, as the following accounts demonstrate.

Working with young children and their incredible intensities and seeing things stretched over a long period of time, and then nothing is ever finished you can keep going, or you can transform it or you can keep working with it. So it's not discrete bits of information that you're trying to convey. In the creating of it there really isn't a stop. Things stop when a child has to go to the bathroom, stops when it's the end of term and there's a two-week break.

> It's seeing learning as this long continuity and I'm in it too. I'm not doing this *for* children, or *for* students but this is as much about my own learning my own engagement as it is theirs. So in a sense, for me, I'm always trying to create these situations where I'm disoriented and I have to figure things out too. That's the pleasure in the work. These long stretches of working things out.
>
> *(Sylvia Kind, interview, November 2020)*

There is a strong sense of the collaborative nature of the knowledge generation or meaning-making that is happening: the studio as a thinking space, a laboratory that gives permission for a particular relationship with time. 'The studio is imagined as a space of collective inquiry that affords both children and educators time to dwell with materials, linger in artistic processes and work together on particular ideas and propositions' (Kind et al. 2019: 67; Pacini-Ketchabaw et al. 2017).

This points to how the studio can be an arena for the *cultivation* rather than *consumption* of knowledge, a concept that links to Froebel's creating of a kindergarten as a place of growth and interconnectedness (for example, Liebschner 1992; Werth 2019).

Sylvia explained further about the collaboration that can take place:

SYLVIA: And I guess that to me is such an important aspect whether you're working with children or with adult students or educators, is this idea of not just using a material or an idea to do something with it. But how do we participate with it, to move with it, to correspond with it which then has huge implications in terms of how we create spaces.

ALISON: How can you create an arena in which that can 'happen?'

SYLVIA: Which is a beautiful puzzle! . . .. to always try to figure out. So, and I think part of slow knowledge to me is what are we cultivating? It's not just what we're thinking about, learning, or doing, but what is being cultivated? What we are cultivating, such as the ways of knowing, the kinds of understandings, and ways of being, matters significantly in the environments, spaces, and situations we create. How we approach things matters, so we're not just addressing knowledge about something, giving information to consume, or using materials for instrumental purposes. Rather, we are cultivating spaces of paying attention, of slowing down so we can notice not just what individuals are doing, but what others are doing so we can engage in it and enter into correspondence with others, materials and ideas.

There is a further dimension that emerged in our discussion in relation to how a studio can hold time. There is something particular about an environment that is visited by many different groups of young children and students in contrast to an early childhood room that becomes the base for one cohort of children over a long period.

The studio has become a creative space where the space itself speaks. If I think about the drawings on the wall, some have been there for 13 years.

Over this time different projects have taken place, various groups of children and their younger siblings have come and gone. I don't keep everything on the walls, but a trace of the history that says other children have been here before and have been thinking about particular things, so children come into a space already alive with ideas. Instead of cleaning it up every year as if you start anew, I think of it as a space that holds history and holds traces and remnants of what has been before. The materials in the space matters.

(Sylvia Kind, interview, November 2020)

This approach demonstrates a way of thinking about how the fabric of a learning environment can hold a history of children's ideas and be a provocation for new enquiries. It is a form of *accumulated* and *collaborative* knowledge that we will return to when thinking about pedagogical documentation (see Chapter 7).

Discussion

Time for generating firsthand knowledge

Experiential, slow ways of knowing as discussed in this chapter pose a particular challenge for early childhood teacher education and professional development if both are carried out within the time-pressured, 'educator as technician' climate discussed in Part 1.

Biljana Fredriksen highlighted the importance of this concrete rather than abstract learning in her interview:

ALISON: And I think what I've picked up from your other responses, in your work with the students . . . you're teaching people through first hand experiences and you're saying that you need to experience this, and this is part of meeting what particular goals the course might have. But actually you need to feel this and that will mean it might be slower than you imagine.

BILJANA: Spot on! I'm also becoming more aware of how important it is that you really push people gently into experiencing something first. And then they come with questions back to you, instead of telling students: 'If you do this, this is going to happen and the clay's going to crack so don't do this' . . .. Nobody remembers it anyway so I say 'It's okay, just do it and then we'll see what cracks and what happens'. Sometimes I give students a little advice. Some of them pick it up, some of them don't. If they don't, that's ok and then, when they experience what happens first hand, it becomes more meaningful talking about it because it is something that concerns them. So they come with their own questions.

There are few substitutes for such firsthand experiences, especially if these explorations are going to inform future pedagogical relationships with children. I am interested in how the pace of these interactions is an important part of the process, as Kari Carlsen explains:

> But this could be difficult for preschool, teachers and staff to grasp: 'What is the value of playing so much with these sticks or 'Why should we use clay? It's so dirty. We could make "playdough" with flour instead because it's cleaner'. I think these slow practices are part of how we connect the children to the natural environment.
>
> *(Kari Carlsen, interview, September 2020)*

Bringing your own self with you

The importance of recognising the value of firsthand experiences in teaching slow practices is also linked to our personal biographies including individual memories of early childhood and learning. We saw earlier in Chapter 3 how Sylvia pointed to her own childhood in reflecting on where she had first come across slow practices.

'Bringing your own self with you' and 'not leaving your own lived experience at the door' resonates with the holistic approach of social pedagogy: 'Social pedagogues bring themselves – "head, heart and hands" – to the work, and see themselves in a personal as well as professional relationship with those they work with' (Cameron et al. 2021: 6; see Chapter 8).

This is echoed by the concept of 'personal pedagogy' (Van Manen 2016: 11) that I discussed at the start of this chapter. Here self-reflection and awareness of our personal backgrounds and identity is examined to impact on how and why we teach. The importance of acknowledging the personal in the professional can also be seen to be relevant when thinking about how slow practices are taught to ECEC students. Biljana drew attention to how students may not have experienced different speeds of learning and maybe unaware of their own preferred ways of acquiring knowledge.

> And then if you go through the schedule, it might fit some of the students, but students are individuals that have different speeds, they have different ways of learning they have different ways of interacting. So, each scheduled timetable will fit someone and not others. Whilst students are in Primary and Secondary school they learn to be obedient, in terms of the schedule. But if the scheduled thinking did not work for them maybe they never learned what it means to take their own initiative? The dilemma is how to manoeuvre around this in teacher education, to still have the lectures, but to also recognise that learning can go at different speeds and to enable students to find their own ways of acquiring knowledge. So when I make a teaching plan, it is a result of my imagining what might be appropriate for this year for these students. And it builds on my past experiences. But I still always have to

keep in mind that these students are different from any other students before. There will be some similarities but I have to be open to change something because things can evolve.

(Biljana Fredriksen, interview, October 2020)

If students' own childhood and school experience have been solely clock-driven and performance-focused then encountering pedagogies that embrace a different relationship with time can be a challenge. Enabling children to explore materials firsthand can introduce an element of uncertainty for educators. There is skill involved in sensing the right moment to hold back or to offer a new material or demonstrate another way of working (Carlsen and Clark 2022). Early childhood teacher education can be a forum for becoming more comfortable with uncertainty and in gaining patience with materials but this can be a frustrating and daunting process, as Tahmina Shayan commented:

Students come into the classroom from different places in the world and some of them have been educated in the 'factory model' of schools. Everything is so rushed and accelerated and they want it to be predictable like this. Thinking of some students, everything has to be stated and when I change something they get so frustrated because they're not okay with change . . .. They don't want to be flexible because they're so afraid of inflexibility. They don't like uncertainty. They become uncomfortable with things when there are unknowns. So for these students, for example, they feel secure when 12 o'clock is lunchtime or 3pm is outdoor time – everybody has to get outside no matter if the children are tired today and if they want to sleep in.

(Tahmina Shayan)

Conclusion

The relationship between time and materials can enable different kinds of thinking, as we have seen through the examples of working with clay and the fallen tree. These materials in turn connect young children to their locality, to the wider world, histories and cultural associations. We have explored several ways of thinking about a studio as a generator of slow knowledge. These discussions have focused on dedicated arts spaces within ECEC but the possibilities raised go beyond these enclosed environments. Perhaps, as we saw in Chapter 5 about slow practices and place, a designed environment can introduce different possibilities of approaches to the clock; however, it is not the environment or the materials in isolation but the bringing together of these different elements, working with a pedagogy that is open to the unexpected and desires an expansive view of time. These explorations continue when we turn next to slow practices and pedagogical documentation.

Questions

1 How do you think your own experience of education as a child and adult has impacted on your approaches to pedagogy and the construction of knowledge?
2 How does paint, drawing or clay, change the relationship with time?
3 What do you think an ECEC environment looks like where educators enjoy 'being in the questions together with children'?

7

SLOW PRACTICES AND PEDAGOGICAL DOCUMENTATION

Introduction

This chapter focuses on the slow practice of pedagogical documentation, as first developed by educators in the Italian city of Emilia (Rinaldi 2005, 2006; Fleet et al. 2017; Merewether 2020). The relationship with time is embedded in the approach to ECEC expressed in the pre-schools in Reggio and is an essential part of a pedagogy that places listening at its centre (Rinaldi 2005, 2006). However, time as a significant 'ingredient' has received less explicit attention in discussions and adaptations of this pedagogical approach than other more visually apparent characteristics, such as recognising the physical environment as a 'third teacher'. Valentine (2006) describes both time and documentation as two of the ways 'in which the Scottish early years education system could learn from the Reggio Approach':

> In many ways, for those considering the adaptation of all areas of the Reggio Approach one of the most important issues for consideration is time. We must consider how we make use of time in practical terms but we must also give consideration to time in philosophical terms.
>
> Time and how children and adults use it, is central to the Reggio philosophy. The rhythm and pace of the child is always given overriding importance. It is given enormous value. In the words of a parent of a Reggio child: '. . . take possession of time as a value, not only as a means to an end. [We must] find and give back meaning to time.'
>
> *(Valentine 2006: 30)*

My aim is to consider the process of pedagogical documentation through a temporal lens (Carlsen and Clark 2022). The discussion that follows will look at the change in tempo or slowing down implicit in this form of documenting learning

DOI: 10.4324/9781003051626-9

but also how different forms of pedagogical documentation can 'hold time' in various ways for children, parents, educators and communities.

Thinking about pedagogical documentation is 'challenging and rewarding' as Formosinho and Peeters (2019: 1) point out. There have been many volumes dedicated to describing pedagogical documentation in its complexity (for example, Giudici and Krechevsky 2001; Fleet et al. 2017; Formosinho and Peeters 2019; Albin-Clark 2020). My aim here is to keep both the *pedagogical intent* or purpose of the documentation and the *relationship with time* in focus.

I will start with an explanation of what pedagogical documentation is as described by Peter Moss in his book *Alternative narratives in early childhood education* in this series:

> Pedagogical documentation can be described as a process of making processes (such as learning) and practices (such as project work) visible and therefore subject to reflection, dialogue, interpretation and critique. It involves, therefore, both documentation itself through the production and selection of varied materials (e.g., photographs, videos, tape recordings, notes, children's work etc.) *and* discussion and analysis of this documentation in a rigorous, critical and democratic way – always in relationship with others.
>
> *(Moss 2019: 85)*

Discussion about pedagogical documentation and time needs to be aware of both *the making* and *discussing* elements of this process. Jane Merewether in this summary reminds us of the collaborative nature of the endeavour:

> The dialogic and emergent nature of the pedagogical documentation process enables researchers to collaborate with young children through sustained interactions, making space for the insights of young children, who are viewed as experts on their own experience, to enrich the research and contribute to its directions (Clark 2017; Fleet et al. 2017; Giamminuti 2013; Merewether 2018; Pacini-Ketchabaw et al. 2015).
>
> *(Merewether 2020: 5)*

Pedagogical documentation as a slow practice

I begin with an extract from my interview with Mara Krechevsky, a senior researcher at Project Zero at Harvard Graduate School of Education whose many years of educational research has included collaborative research with educators in Reggio Emilia in the Making Learning Visible study (Giudici and Krechevsky 2001).

> I think one of the main benefits or outcomes of the process of documenting learning is getting [educators] to slow down, listen, and observe. I think

listening and observing are at the heart of why it's so important to slow down as well . . .. the French philosopher Simone Weil said, 'Attention is the rarest and purest form of generosity'. I've always loved this notion. Some of the teachers I've worked with have talked about the importance of deciding 'where are you going to focus yourattention?' Documentation supports reflection on teaching and learning by acknowledging that you can't take everything in in the moment itself. So, you're going to miss a lot of things in the teaching and learning setting. And to avoid depending on just what rises to the surface, in terms of what you remember, it's important to have some kind of record or documentation of what the kids said or their work so that you can go back and then look at it again . . .

Here's another really important part of why it's so important to slow down. We all bring our own subjectivity to whatever it is that we're looking at. I don't think that's a problem – it's a strength because we are drawing on the experiences and knowledge that we've gained, but it's still just one perspective. In order to gather other perspectives you need the documentation. It also allows you to bring in other subjectivities. The documentation should provide a basis for others to agree or disagree with your subjective interpretation of whatever you've collected and enable someone to say, 'Well, I actually don't agree that that child was demonstrating critical thinking because . . .' and point to the documentation as a shared point of reference.

(Mara Krechevsky, interview, October 2020)

Mara Krechevsky's comments are a helpful way of thinking about the relationship between pedagogical documentation and time. Choosing where to focus your attention as an educator is an important professional step and pedagogical documentation can give educators permission to grasp a moment that has held a child's or group of children's attention and to stay with it, running alongside as the children's ideas develop.

Compiling a visual and verbal record of these learning moments can 'freeze time' in a specific way. Instead of educators and children holding an individual memory of an event or sequence of moments, pedagogical documentation can become a shared record. It is therefore entangled with time. As Mara comments: 'Documentation supports reflection on teaching and learning by acknowledging that you can't take everything in in the moment itself.' It is not just a question of not being able to hold onto everything we have experienced but that our first impressions may benefit from a deeper reflection beyond the first glance. This looking and thinking again may also benefit from being open to other perspectives. The documentation may, as Mara indicates, provide the opportunity for others to agree or disagree with our first impressions and importantly for children and their peers to be fully part of this process.

This links to Carlina Rinaldi's description of a 'pedagogy of listening' which contains three different but related concepts of listening: internal listening, which is the individual time for 'thinking what you think'; multiple listening, which opens up to the perspectives of others; and visible listening, which creates a tangible record of this process (Rinaldi 2005, 2006).

The investment in time is embedded in each of these types of listening: the internal self-reflection, gathering multiple perspectives and the documenting of such exchanges. There is not a rush to give a complete, one-dimensional account but the confidence to open out the narrative for others to contribute:

> The documenter looks at the events that have taken place with a personal view aimed at a deep understanding of them and, at the same time, seeks communicative clarity. This is possible (although it could seem paradoxical) by bringing into the documentation the sense of incompleteness and expectation that can arise when you try to offer others not what you know, but the boundaries of your knowledge; that is, your limits, which derive from the fact that the 'object' being narrated is a process and a path of research.
>
> *(Rinaldi 2006: 71)*

The philosopher Simone Weil's comment that Mara referred to, describes deep attention as a form of generosity. This is not a quality that is often made explicit in pedagogical terms. I think the generosity that is called for here in relation to pedagogical documentation is the ability to pause from making a swift assessment of what is happening. Rinaldi refers to this when she discusses the ability to be willing 'to offer others not what you know but the boundaries of your knowledge' (2006: 71). This calls for an openness to many possibilities and at the same time a deliberate setting aside of other agendas, professional and personal, in order to focus with full attention on what the children you are working with are doing and saying. The qualities of generosity and humility are linked. It is perhaps a demonstration of 'epistemological humility' (Clark 2010a: 190; Clark and Flewitt 2020), where an educator or researcher is able to be curious and to be comfortable with not knowing. This may be far more challenging in some cultural contexts than in others.

Different forms of pedagogical documentation and time

This next section aims to provoke ongoing discussion about viewing pedagogical documentation through a temporal lens, drawing on conversations in my interviews. This includes brief reflections on the processes of pedagogical documentation in New Zealand, Scotland and Norway. Each is connected in some way to the concept of pedagogical documentation as originated in the pre-schools of Reggio Emilia, but with different narratives attuned to local contexts and developed in sometimes diverse directions.

Learning stories

There is an echo here of an earlier book I co-edited with Peter Moss and the Norwegian academic Anne-Trine Kjørholt (Clark et al. 2005). This book brought together accounts by researchers, educators and policy-makers to look critically at the concept and practice of listening to young children. The New Zealand early childhood academics, Margaret Carr, Carolyn Jones and Wendy Lee discuss in their chapter how listening to children's voices can be part of assessment practice that is based on a narrative methodology:

> Learning Stories are a method of documenting everyday interactions. Most of them include a learning episode, a 'short -term review' and a 'what next?' . . .. In this method, the assessments – and the notions of valuable knowledge and competence that they take as reference points – have called on multiple perspectives. Assessment records that include stories (that can be revisited) and photographs (that can be read by the children).
>
> *(Carr et al. 2005: 141)*

There are several features of this early description of Learning Stories that appear to me to signify the important temporal dimensions to this form of documentation. An interest in children's 'everyday interactions' places the focus in the moment and the phrase 'short-term review' also suggests the desire for this documentation to be of value in the present whilst 'what next?' opens up a shared discussion about the future. The acknowledgement of the importance of revisiting signals that it is recognised time is needed for this documentation process. This is not about gathering instant responses that subsequently disappear from view.

The three key elements of assessment referred to in this same chapter were 'noticing, recognising and responding' (Cowie and Carr 2004) that has subsequently been expanded to include recording and revisiting, as Amanda Bateman discussed in her interview:

> Bronwyn Cowie talks about this *notice, recognise* and *respond* to this systematic way of working with children. And I absolutely think this does slow things down and you've got this systematic way of looking at your own practice, *noticing*. So when you're observing, when I think about teachers sitting in sand pits and watching children just being there being present for children, being able to notice something that's going on with the children that you think this could potentially be a really interesting learning moment for that child, they are clearly interested in it so noticing and *recognising* this as a learning moment that there is this potential, it has affordances or [the opportunity for] pedagogical exchange to go on here. And the *respond* is the thing that I'm really interested in, because it's often what students are confused about . . . how do you actually respond?'
>
> So you've seen this thing going on, it could be between a group of children, or two children together, or a child alone, but how do you actually enter into a discourse into a conversation with that child into an interaction with that child where you can help to support some sort of learning that's happening there? . . . .. And *recording* and *revisiting* them so . . . you're writing

the Learning Story, *recording* of the learning that actually happened there and then *revisiting* that with the child, whenever they want to. So sitting down and looking at the Learning Story books with children. And I think this is really key to actually unpacking that learning for them and for them to be reflective learners as well.

(Amanda Bateman, interview, September 2020)

Again, we can see in Amanda's reflections the temporal dimensions to this form of documentation, including the implicit necessity of educators slowing down in order to notice, recognise, respond, record and revisit. Margaret Carr and Wendy Lee have written subsequently about the relationship with time in Learning Stories and portfolios, drawing on Jay Lemke's work about timescales: 'Everywhere in human culture we find . . . longer term processes and shorter term events linked by a material object that functions in both cases semiotically as well as materially' (Lemke 2000: 281 cited in Carr and Lee 2019: 22). Building on this understanding Carr and Lee describe Learning Stories as short-term events that are connected to long-term processes held in the portfolios.

Lived stories

Pedagogical documentation can be understood as part of resistance to dominant narratives of measurement (Dahlberg et al. 2013; Moss 2019). Lynn McNair describes how Lived Stories originated. This is a particular form of pedagogical documentation, developed with a team of Scottish researchers and educators (McNair et al. 2021; Blaisdell et al. 2021). This form of documentation that was developed both challenged and operated within the existing policy and administrative structures:

> First, that the Lived Stories were indeed seen by practitioners as a way to deconstruct and resist reductive, top-down assessment of children. Second, we examine the ways that the Lived Stories remained embedded in 'the system', meddling with rather than eliminating – the local authority systems.
>
> *(McNair et al. 2021: 485)*

Lynn explained her understanding of the relationship with the New Zealand model of Learning Stories, discussed in this chapter:

> Well, I will say that our Lived Stories work we were documenting the everyday moments of children so, and our lived stories, built on Margaret Carr and Wendy Lee's Learning Stories. But . . . our stories, we hope capture the civic life of the child as well. So one example, a quick example would be that one day, a member of staff was serving lunches, and there was a child crying behind them, and she went over to speak to the child, and you know this child was having a difficult time at home. Her Mum was quite ill, and I think

information was being kept from her rather than shared with her. And so she was worrying a lot. But the member of staff thought, and we actually had held a meeting about it, because we were actually thinking, we were using the Learning Stories way of documenting learning. And then, we said, 'Actually this is more than a learning moment, this is their lived experiences'. So that's where we kind of changed that. So it was about these everyday moments that are not necessarily learning. But they are definitely about that.

I've said here also seizing the discursive events of everyday life. These moments that are critical for the children. And also our Lived Stories help us engage with the kinds of tensions and uncertainties of learning, because you're . . . tuning into the child, and capturing that and then of course you're applying sophisticated analysis to it. And then . . . a possible provocation. So there are no real ends, it's like capturing the complexity of that child.

(Lynn McNair, September 2020)

Lived Stories, in common with the other forms of pedagogical documentation discussed in this chapter, can be seen as a way of gathering slow knowledge with young children that respects their cultural identity. Lynn continued:

This is a big thing for me; it's a view I am really passionate about, how knowledge is acquired slowly through cultural maturation . . .. We notice that we've got a lot of children from a variety of different places, and we notice that in some cultures, things aren't as valued as they are in England, or Scotland or Britain, but actually those children are really great at other things. And I think that that's another problem with 'fast knowledge'. I think knowledge should be shaped within children's cultural context.

The time taken to gather detailed narratives of everyday encounters in the early childhood centre was an issue that caused tension with some educators deciding to write up the Lived Stories at home which would not be a recommended or sustainable option (McNair et al. 2021: 487).

Discussion

I would like to discuss two aspects of the relationship between pedagogical documentation, purpose and time: the longer-term value of documentation for young children and the danger of documentation becoming solely about performance and display.

Pedagogical documentation and its value over time for young children

I want to return here to the question of pedagogical documentation and timescales (Carr and Lee 2019). The portfolios described by Carr and Lee held a longer timescale than the Learning Stories. Portfolios could be a point of contact for young children with past events that could also be a source of comfort in the present and into the future. Driscoll and Rudge (2005) described a similar effect of the children's profile books, as developed in their early childhood centre in London. The profile books were seen as documents of the 'real lived and living culture of the child's life' (Driscoll and Rudge 2005: 96). Compiled with young children and with parents, the books became an accumulative 'living' record of children's interests, achievements and concerns. One example stands out for me. Driscoll and Rudge describe how from a young age Toby needed to be given daily medication which he hated (Driscoll and Rudge 2005: 97–98).

> He would scream and cry and refuse. At the nursery Toby's key worker decided that it would be good to work through this with Toby. He was, at the time, only one-and-a-half years old. Photos were taken of the whole process starting with the medicines, then the key worker getting them ready, then of Toby crying having his medication. Then this was then put into his profile book. This was a big breakthrough for Toby, as we would talk through this daily with him. The wording of the pictures in the profile book was short and to the point, for example, 'Toby does not like having his medicine', 'Toby is crying', 'He is sad'.
>
> *(Driscoll and Rudge 2005: 97)*

It is not possible to convey in this short extract the care and sensitivity that was involved in this process. The purpose of this documentation, I understand to be, was not to hide from Toby his distress but to gradually enable him to have more control over the process. Toby's profile book became an important part of his coping with this experience, and provided a catalyst for conversations between Toby, his peers, the educators and his parents. Over time his confidence grew until: '. . . with great pride we could add the final picture to the medicine incident and that was Toby giving himself the actual medicine, smiling' (Driscoll and Rudge 2005: 97).

This embodied record connects with the Lived Stories described by Lynn McNair earlier in this chapter.

Pedagogical documentation can also have a value on a longer timescale at a group or class level as well as for individual children. This reminded me of a flip chart I noticed in a nursery class in Correggio, Northern Italy. The class had been developing their own vocabulary, an elaborate series of signs and symbols. When the children reached the end of the academic year this pedagogical documentation moved together with the children to their next class. It was recognised as accumulated, slow knowledge (see Chapter 6) that was an important record of past collaboration and a potential springboard for future explorations. I see this as representing a longer view of time where value is given to past discoveries as well as current endeavours. It is an appreciation of 'old knowledge' (Orr 1996; See Chapter 4) and shared knowledge beyond individual achievement. How different this feels from approaches to transitions for young children that, perhaps unintentionally, may wipe any trace of past endeavours away: new displays; new records; new books. It is a reminder that children's preoccupations and concerns can extend across year groups and may exist along different tracks from the prescribed curriculum. I will return to this question of 'time travel' through documentation in Chapter 10 when I explore slow practices and research, thinking about how documentation can support children to return to past events and to reconnect it with the present and future.

The relationship between time and education includes a consideration of how memories are stored, both individual and collective. So, in a system where measurement becomes the dominant culture, what can be measured becomes the features that are preserved, and other facets of early childhood may become less visible on the timetable and perhaps on the walls.

Memories can be stored in classrooms, in paper portfolios and in digital spaces. A key question for me is: how involved are children in what is made visible and what relationship can children continue to have with these artefacts? Kate Cowan and Rosie Flewitt have explored this topic in detail (for example, Cowan and Flewitt 2021). Exploring the increasing 'e-portfolios' and 'online-learning journals', Cowan and Flewitt highlight the possibilities opened up by these forms of digital documentation including the ability to capture moving images and sound. At the same time they point to how the adult-orientated design may make it harder for children to contribute to and feel ownership of such documentation.

Documentation as performance and display?

Documentation can lose sight of the child or children. It can become an end point – a goal in itself – a justification for what has been achieved rather than a process and a springboard for future explorations. Rinaldi emphasises how pedagogical documentation 'is not a documentation of products but of processes, of mental paths' (2005: 100). An increasingly measured culture in ECEC can be seen as one of the external pressures that can impact on the form that documentation takes. Commenting on UK policy and practice, Fawcett and Watson caution: 'The pressure to document for external bodies (funders, managers, schools) is important to remember in our increasingly performance-managed educational and social worlds' (Fawcett and Watson 2016: 185).

Mari Mori commented on these external pressures to document in this way her experience of working with ECEC educators in Japan:

> When it comes to documentation many of them tell us there isn't time to do documentation and to talk about it with children so it can be *pedagogical* documentation. My contacts with kindergartens and kindergarten teachers are saying this. And I think they take a lot of photos but for the parents because they had such things as 'My kid' I think it's an app, and they do it every day actually and it takes a lot of time. I wonder if the parents are so very

interested in it. But then they can then say we have done the right thing. So that's the sort of evidence.

(Mari Mori, interview, September 2020)

Pedagogical documentation can, under these pressures, become life-less rather than dynamic and alive. This can result in the process being seen as merely for decoration or display. Documentation in this context may cease to be part of daily pedagogical exploration between children and educators and instead become an end in itself. The chief audience has become external (Bath 2012). A further concern if documentation loses its pedagogical value is that it can be 'time-consuming' – in the sense of eating up valuable pedagogical time, as Deborah Harcourt discussed with me:

DEBORAH: If you look at documentation for example, some people have the parent as the audience rather than saying: '. . . I slow my documentation down to inform my own practice, to make me a better teacher, for me to understand my work and the children.'

I was working with an Early Childhood setting last year, who had a four-year degree trained early childhood educator full time on the computer all day, uploading all of their pieces on StoryPark and Facebook, etc., and parents on the phone at three o'clock saying 'There's no photos of my child uploaded' . . . I explained 'the regulations don't tell you to do that . . . But it's a marketing strategy for the privatised early childhood in Australia, There's no engagement with the material.' Not 'Why have I chosen this photograph?', why have I chosen this story?', 'why am I . . .' It's just uploaded and its done so there's no slowing in that process either.

ALISON: So it's not pedagogical . . .

DEBORAH: No, it's marketing. Nothing to do with pedagogy at all.

Such documentation may have an instant purpose but does not hold a longer-term pedagogical value and can place the educator in a role as technician. It seems in sharp contrast to the form of pedagogical documentation discussed by Sylvia Kind in the studio in Chapter 6, where the walls hold a history, hold traces and the materials matter, acting as catalysts for new directions.

Conclusion

The aim of this chapter has been to focus on the purpose of pedagogical documentation and the relationship with time. These forms of living record, of assessment and exchange can slow down everyday practices so events in the moment can be returned to by educators, children and parents. Pedagogical documentation can also demonstrate longevity by travelling with individual children as they grow and with groups of children as a form of 'visible listening' (Rinaldi 2005: 22) that holds accumulated knowledge.

I would like to end this chapter with Christina MacRae, Abigail Hackett and Rachel Holmes summary (2020) of the value of pedagogical documentation in relation to time drawing on the work of Hillev Lenz Taguchi:

> Pedagogical documentation offers a tool that allows us to think more deeply about time in that it 'maps out a fraction of a learning event and makes it materialise before us in the documentation' (Lenz Taguchi 2010: 60). Not only does the documentation make visible the singularity of the event as it unfolds, it also shifts our attention to the way that adults respond to these moments.
>
> *(MacRae et al, 2020, p. 241)*

Questions

1   In what ways does time impact on the process of pedagogical documentation?
2   Pedagogical documentation can be time-consuming. Who do you see as the main audience?
3   How can slowing down pedagogical documentation support next steps with children?

8

SLOW PRACTICES AND THE EVERYDAY

Introduction

Slow practices and the everyday in ECEC draws on pedagogical, cultural and philosophical concerns. Mealtimes represent one of these meeting points and will be among the themes explored with a temporal lens in this chapter. This brings us back to the Slow Food movement and the emphasis on the pleasure of eating meals together, incorporating the nutritional with the social (Honoré 2004). Particular attention will be given to the relevance of slow practices with the youngest children in ECEC.

The Danish concept of valuing the mundane in everyday life (Jensen 2011, 2017) and the concept of pedagogues as 'experts in everyday life' (Cameron and Moss 2011; Cameron 2020; Cameron et al. 2021) provides one strand to this dialogue. Jytte Jensen writing about Danish pedagogical practice in the context of a cross-national study explains:

> Everyday life activities, such as having a meal, going to the bathroom, sleeping and so on, are emphasised not only in Danish pedagogical work with young children but also in the pedagogical work with other groups, such as children and young people in residential care and adults with severe disabilities living in shared accommodation. In all such settings, these activities take up much time and space. The great importance given to the everyday life in Danish centres also underlines the importance attached to the life here and now instead of instrumental ideas about future outcomes. What is important – what matters – is children and adults living together.
>
> *(Jensen 2011: 149)*

I had the opportunity to be part of a research team working with Jytte Jensen and colleagues as part of a European project, Care Work in Europe: Current

DOI: 10.4324/9781003051626-10

Understandings and Future Directions (Cameron and Moss 2007). The study focused on care work across the life course. One element of this cross-national study involved compiling half-hour films of pedagogical practice in early childhood centres in Denmark, England and Hungary as a stimulus for discussion among educators (or pedagogues in the case of Denmark). The methodological framework developed during this study became known as SOPHOS (Second Order Phenomenological Observation Scheme (Hansen and Jensen 2004), inspired by and adapted from the video-cued ethnography of Tobin et al. (1989, 2009).

The following extract is an observation from the subsequent study that Jensen carried out with Danish pedagogues who watched the films from the three countries:

> According to the following statement by an academic in pedagogy, the practice in the English film shows the meals are pieces of everyday life to which no particular attention is paid: 'What really stands out is the lack of involvement in everyday situations in [the English film]. The Danish centre is based on an everyday approach. We bring food and plates to and fro. It is a project that goes on alongside everything else. In [the English film] it is all about other things, and about learning stuff.
>
> As the pedagogues saw it, eating as well as visits to the toilet seem to be of less import[ance], the consequence being that the staff are simply servicing the children.
>
> *(Jensen 2011: 148)*

This is one external comment and not intended as a universally applied judgement, but the reflection 'it is all about other things' seems to raise a key question here. What value is given to the everyday practices in ECEC in different contexts? I suggest that the pace and attention given to such routines is closely linked to this question of perceived value. There is a rich stream of philosophical and sociological thought that considers the concept of the everyday. Sherringham (2006) describes everydayness as rooted in the practices that make the everyday visible. The Australian early childhood researchers Suallyn [Mitchelmore], Sheila Degotardi and Alma Fleet Mitchelmore (2017; Mitchelmore 2021) engage with the concept of 'le quotidien' identified as 'the dimension of lived experience that is involved in everyday life' (Sherringham 2006: 2). Drawing in particular on the work of the French sociologist and educational thinker Lefebvre (1991, 2013). Mitchelmore and colleagues demonstrate 'the potentiality of everyday moments' with the youngest children in ECEC through a sequence of narratives that involve children's connection with feeding bibs (2017: 92–95). It feels in these beautifully constructed narratives that the pace of interaction has been slowed down almost to a standstill in order to give full attention to these moments. One such encounter involved a group of young children between 18 months and 2 years choosing which bibs to wear:

> Christopher was taking his time, pondering his decision. It was not that he did not know which feeding bib he wanted but more that Christopher

seemed to enjoy the process of choice. His finger firmly indicated the bib with the lion print and Beth, the educator within this moment, warmly confirmed with him, 'You'd like the lions . . . OK.

(Mitchelmore et al. 2017: 92)

This chapter will move from routines to rhythms to moments. We will examine different examples of slowing down the everyday but also consider how this attention to pace can also involve the capacity to be spontaneous. This will take us from the planned to the unplanned.

We start sitting around a table sharing a meal.

Routines

Thinking again about the aims of the Slow Food movement, one of the characteristics is to take pleasure in eating together with friends and family (Honoré 2004: 52). The Slow food manifesto states:

A firm defence of quiet material pleasure is the only way to oppose the universal folly of Fast Life . . .. Our defence should begin at the table with Slow food.

(Honoré 2004: 52–53)

So the table is maybe another helpful place to begin to think about the value of slow practices and the relationship with time in early childhood education.

There are two examples about mealtimes in this chapter: one is an initiative that has taken place in a group of early childhood centres in Australia and the second is an example of developing practice in Falkirk, Scotland. Both initiatives were unaware of each other but there are many parallels between the two projects, in terms of their starting points and approaches.

Beginning with the table – rethinking the 'rush hour'

When I'm working with early learning centres now, that's where I start with the 'eleven to two' (o'clock). How can we make practice changes in that period of time where we slow everything down, where children have genuine choices about transforming tables that had playdough on them ten minutes earlier. So really slowing that practice down and having children engaged in the whole slow process themselves so they become responsible for transforming the tables, resetting the tables for lunch so a new friend can come along and making sure that the children are self-serving their own food.

(Deborah Harcourt, interview, October 2020)

As Deborah Harcourt explains one of the catalysts for her project was to consider what the everyday experiences were like for young children who were in 'long daycare' for up to 12 hours a day. Despite the many hours some of the children spent in these centres, Deborah became aware of the hurried nature of lunchtimes. There was a sense of rush to make a rapid transition between the morning activities and lunch with tables being quickly prepared by adults and then lunch delivered to the children. The mealtimes had become mechanistic, an interruption to the rest of the day and a task to be ticked off and completed as quickly as possible.

What we can see in Deborah's description of the change is that in slowing down the lunch time there was the opportunity for young children to be fully engaged in the process of mealtimes over an extended period of the day. There was the chance for children to play an active part in the preparation of the space as well as in serving themselves. The lunchtimes had more opportunity to be experienced as a social time with the chance for adults and children to sit and talk together. There was a different rhythm created to this part of the day and this in turn had a 'ripple' effect, spreading out to have a positive effect on the relationship with time during other parts of the day. Deborah continued:

> And we're talking about matching how your body's feeling with how much you eat, and then we lead that into rest time. And children need to manage that as part of self-regulation as well. Let's slow that right down so children in the centres that I work with now make a choice between 'my body needs a short rest', 'a long rest' or 'a sleep'. So, again, slowing that process down so that the children are engaging with that time rather than being forced to sleep. This is how I started with the lunch and sleep period and then expanded on either side of that eleven to two [o'clock]. How could we slow the welcome down in the morning? How could we have a morning meeting that enabled a large block of uninterrupted time for children? So we were really trying to look at the day in much larger chunks where the practices could be much slower throughout that period of time.
>
> *(Deborah Harcourt)*

Here you can see how focusing attention on mealtimes and allowing a slower pace opened up further opportunities for young children to play a more active role in deciding on everyday routines such as rest times that were intimately linked to the rhythms of their own bodies. Thinking about mealtimes and rest times then led to a reassessment about how time was approached in other periods of the day, such as the welcome period in the morning. Deborah mentions looking at how 'a large block of uninterrupted time' for the children could be achieved, echoing Cuffaro's phrase 'unfragmented time' (see Chapter 3).

The second example is the Marvellous Meals project that began in early childhood centres in Falkirk, a Scottish local authority. This initiative was established in response to a change in early years policy in Scotland to extend the number of hours of funding available for early learning and childcare (ELC) for every three- and four-year-old and eligible two-year-old children. The entitlement was increased to 1,140 hours or 30 hours a week if taken in term time. This initiative is referred to in the sector as '1,140 hours'. Donna Green, a member of my focus group, explained further in response to hearing about Deborah's 'rush hour':

> Deborah's research . . . resonated really nicely with us as we had started what we call 'Marvellous meals'. It started off as a very small test of change . . . when nursery classes went from two and a half hours to offering the full day nine till three. I think a lot of management felt the children would just go to the dining room, they would go for the half hour, the one- to three-year-olds. It was a very rushed and it didn't work and so from that they had to think about, 'Right, lets really look at the children here. What's working?' So we're really taking it back and it resonated really strongly when I was reading the research . . . because we started with the Lunchtime period as well, for staff that whole principle and part of what they're doing, so just that bit about children can take their time, they can make the food in the morning, they can go to the larder, they can grow it. And really slow it all down and really allow the child to lead when they're going for lunch when they're going for snack instead of it being really rushed. It's taken a long time, I think this is only the third year, but we are seeing a huge difference by starting with looking at that middle of the day, really looking at practice and thinking about our principles and the child's voice and allowing them to be part of it and own it. It's their lunch!
>
> (Donna Green, focus group, April 2021)

The relationship with time is evident in several ways in this example of developing practice, underpinned by Froebelian principles (for example, Bruce 2020; see Chapter 3). The necessity for the change came about as a result of a new early years policy that funded more hours for young children to be in nursery provision (Paterson 2022). So in a literal sense there was suddenly more time but these extra hours did not automatically lead to changes in the organisation of routines that could benefit the children. It was only after observing how the youngest children struggled with the rushed routine at lunchtime in the school dining hall, sitting in a large and unfamiliar space to eat their lunch within a restricted timeframe, that routines were imaginatively rethought. Donna draws attention to how educators found that restructuring mealtimes and slowing down the process increased the opportunity to talk to children during mealtimes, helping to create a social experience rather than viewing eating as refuelling.

Subsequently 'Marvellous mealtimes' has become a way to integrate opportunities for young children to grow and prepare food. Here children can experience firsthand the different timescales involved in making a meal, from growing carrots to boiling pasta.

There can be seen a direct link between this practical approach and Froebel's emphasis on young children's immersion in everyday activities including gardening, as testified by the named individual plots in the garden for children as well as their responsibility for a collective plot in Froebel's kindergarten at Blankenberg (Tovey 2017: 1–13).

Rhythms

Deborah's account of lunchtimes also raised the topic of children's sleep patterns. This is a specific area where the relationship with the clock is interconnected with the rhythms of children's bodies. It can highlight some of the tensions between 'institutional time' that follows a predesigned, linear schedule and children's 'body clock' and family patterns.

The question of tuning into young children's rhythms was discussed in my focus group. The following comments are by Liz Turbitt, an early childhood educator and student with experience working with babies:

> I mean babies are fascinating to watch and see where they're going and what are they doing and their interactions and what they can do it's incredible when you give them time, you have all these babies just doing their own thing organically and they interact and they, they do so much more than we think that they can do but it's about being slow, it's about no rush, no pressure and there always seems to be another snack time or another lunchtime or feeding time it's like they're doing something they're exploring and the next thing they're lifted to have a nappy done it's distressing.
>
> I've really found that as a student that was a bit difficult because you try and model what you want but you don't want to step in and say, 'Where are you going, What's the rush?' and that real respect I think as well for children that really listening to children to tune into them. So, I would always ask a child whatever age, if they wanted their nappy changed, or what I was going to do, not just lift them. I mean imagine in the middle of playing and somebody just [sweeps you up]. What is going on? So that was that whole respect and slowness and real interaction and that communication that you do get with children right from birth, this slow listening.
>
> I think for me, especially working with babies, it's about just **being,** you know, not moving on to the next thing, it's like just enjoying what they're doing, you know, whether that's changing a nappy whether that's having lunch whatever it is they're doing just enjoying that because they're just developing, and there's a real pressure for like to get on to the next thing. But what is the next thing? There is no next thing . . . it's like, that's their day, and the longer they can spend, even a very young child having their lunch in front of them . . . there's no hurry to get it into them. They need to explore it, they need to eat with their hands if that be it you know but they need to just have time. And there's such a pressure at the moment.
>
> *(Liz Turbitt, focus group, April 2021)*

I find Liz's challenge: 'But what is the next thing?' a powerful one that encapsulates a way of engaging with young children that values the here and now and of educators who are comfortable with giving full attention to what is happening. It speaks of a 'timefullness' discussed in Chapter 3.

Moments

The examples so far in this chapter have considered slow practices in ECEC in relation to routines and rhythms. I would like to introduce a third connected element
here: moments. Making the relationship with time more explicit raises questions
about the planned and the unplanned so I want to next disrupt our thinking to
consider the ability to be spontaneous. The Cambridge English dictionary definition is a 'happening or done in a natural, often sudden way, without any planning
or without being forced.'

'Moments' was a word that appeared in several interviews and during discussion
in the online reading group:

> to be **aware** of the moments. We are given moments for common interest
> and learning – to learn to be slow with the environment and to be aware of
> the moments given you as a teacher.
>
> *(Kari Carlsen, interview, September 2020)*

In order to be **aware** of the moments educators need to be attentive to these
opportunities, these gifts. But at the same time the educational system and pedagogy need to be sufficiently 'open weave' enough to allow such moments to be
recognised. If the whole day is tightly structured and timetabled there are less
opportunities to 'go off track', to wander with the children for fear of losing one's
place. There may be external and internal pressures that increase this fear, as discussed in Chapter 2.

How might these moments appear? It can be the environment that presents
these moments. This might be in the form of sudden rain or the sound of thun-
der or the noticing of a season changing as leaves are blown into the classroom.
Moments may be on different scales. Amanda Bateman reflected on one of her
research projects with educators in ECEC in New Zealand:

> [This was] the earthquake project where teachers intentionally embrace
> everything that happened around the earthquake because they deliberately
> weren't going to shy away from it and try and avoid the subject when chil-
> dren wanted to talk about it.
>
> I turned up one day to do some videoing and the head teacher of the early
> childhood centre said to me, 'And just to make this a really authentic visit for
> you, Mandy, we have no water!'
>
> . . .. And so, because we didn't have water the teachers decided, 'right
> so what we're going to do today is we're going to have an investigation and
> we're going to have a walk down the road and see what's happened.' The
> teachers were talking to the children asking: 'Have you heard anything about
> it?' and then the children would give their knowledge about what they've
> heard about this situation so [the educators] are valuing their opinion from
> the offset about what was going on. Then the educators' said 'well let's go

and have a look. Somebody said they thought a lorry had hit something down the road. Right let's go out and have a look.' Then they got ready and walked down the road . . .

And materiality I think where this comes in is, so straightaway you see a wall that's broken completely, you know demolished, one of the teachers says to the child, talking to a group of children that they have 'Oh look at this wall!' to make a noticing of this environmental feature: 'What do you think has happened here?' and then this prompts this discussion these working theories about what they think has happened with this wall, and immediately you get somebody talking about the earthquake, 'I think it was from the earthquake.' 'Oh, . . . how do you think the earthquake has done this?' So there was this lovely exploration of what they thought has happened but it's this materiality this going out and seeing things and having this noticing of a particular environmental feature and the materials within the environment that you can prompt, talk about, I think that's what was key because it then had this lovely pivotal feature of what has happened to that wall now today, where we are present, and one of the children said 'Oh my wall at home is broken down' and so it started this whole conversation about her experience of the earthquake. So these environmental features, drawing attention to them was really important but again it's about the talk around that.

(Amanda Bateman, interview, September 2020)

Not all unplanned events are as momentous as an earthquake. Thinking on a different scale a moment might come in the form of an object brought by a child in their pocket – for example, a leaf, a toy, or an insect. Kari Carlsen related this to a Norwegian term 'dead mouse pedagogy', a phrase referred to in preschool teacher training 30 years ago – taking the moment to follow the children's interests. But this is not necessarily the case in contemporary Norwegian practice, as Solveig Nordtømme commented:

I think they have less time to do what they want to do or choose to do or start to do on impulse because there are too many activities that are planned for the next half an hour, 'we will do this and this.' So there are not so many gaps in time to do what 'I', as a child just want to do, because of the planning by adults.

Maybe the pandemic has changed this situation, but I think that every-thing focuses on the schedule. There are no extended periods when they can choose.

(Solveig Nordtømme, interview, September 2020)

Following unplanned moments can create common interest. This can move the emphasis from individual learning to developing a shared body of knowledge as we heard about happening in the studio (Chapter 6). However, there can be a tension between the planned and unplanned where schedules have become overcrowded or fragmented.

Discussion

The potentiality of moments

Recognising the potential of everyday moments seems to be central to thinking about a slow pedagogy. We have seen in the accounts of changes to mealtimes and in reflecting on daily routines with babies that these markers through the day can be viewed in different ways. Drawing on a social pedagogy tradition, as described by Jensen in relation to Danish pedagogical practice at the start of this chapter, mealtimes and nappy changing can be viewed as an event rather than an interruption to the rest of the day. There is an important temporal dimension to this change of emphasis. It requires a different relationship with the clock. But the slowing down is not intended as the destination but as a gateway to other possibilities including deepening children's relationships with adults and with their peers. Caroline Guard (2021) in her research into social encounters in ECEC between babies and educators refers to the importance of '*adagio interactions*' to promote slow rhythmic dialogic interactions between babies and educators. This connects to the concept of 'presence':

> We began to appreciate presence as deep listening, of being open beyond one's preconceptions and historical ways of making sense. We came to see the importance of letting go of old identities and the need to control.
>
> *(Senge et al. 2008: 13 cited in Horsley 2021: 439)*

Karen Horsley (2021) draws on this concept in her study using documentary photography as a tool for educators to reflect on ECEC practice (see Chapter 10). She describes how working with photography as a form of visual storytelling can slow down the everyday, creating 'photographs that invite questions' (Pardo with Golbach, 2018). But could these slow practices be seen to be creating a form of slow knowledge? Mitchelmore and colleagues make the case for these everyday experiences adding to an 'epistemology of care':

> This means that when one re-encounters an everyday experience, such as mopping the floor, folding the washing or serving lunch, the resonance of past moments persists and through potentiality of the present, care is born *in the moment*. Moments offer us a way to re-examine the overlooked aspects of care. The intention of focusing on 'moments' is not to isolate a single interaction but to pause and project the multiplicity and intersubjectivity of care within the moment.
>
> *(Mitchelmore et al. 2017: 91)*

Slow knowledge assembled in the everyday with young children can lead to a dynamic understanding of what care is about: 'Care is born in the moment.' But to continue to think with Lefebvre's ideas in Rhythmanalysis (2013), Mitchelmore and colleagues point out how such moments are connected across time: 'Moments are not an anchored event; rather they are a duration, resonating and reverberating across days, weeks and years, shaping the culture of spaces' (Mitchelmore et al. 2017: 91).

This attentive approach raises questions about how educators can help to bring such new knowledge constructed during these moments into ongoing interactions with young children and their families. We will return to this question of the relationship between past and present in Chapters 10 and 11.

Exploring slow practices and the everyday has the potential to be a hopeful dialogue in ECEC. It can make us sensitive to where these moments are already happening and celebrate and protect such encounters. Povey et al. (2021) make a similar point when reflecting on their innovation projects in primary school:

> In offering these examples drawn from interruptions of practice, it is important to assert that not only do they offer examples of what could be, but also can sensitise us to recognise moments when *expansive time* is already found – all be it often in fleeting moments.
>
> *(Povey et al. 2021: 121)*

Conclusions

We have seen in this chapter how the relationship with time is deeply embedded in everyday practices in ECEC. Different temporalities or timescapes (Adam 2000) can merge when regulated institutional linear time frames intersect with young children's rhythms. Routines can be viewed as necessary but perhaps annoying interruptions before 'the next thing' or as events in their own right that have value or to refer to Jardine's phrase, can be seen by educators and their colleagues and by parents as 'worth-while time' (Jardine 2008). We have raised the possibility of slow practices in the everyday offering gateways to deeper relationships and to see how 'pedagogically documented moments' (Mitchelmore et al. 2017) can increase our understandings of care as a way to enrich present and future interactions with young children.

Questions

1   How can young children play a more active role in everyday routines in ECEC? How might this affect the role of educators?
2   In what ways might children with special needs benefit from a less hurried approach to everyday routines?
3   What factors prevent more room being given to the unplanned and spontaneous among the planned in ECEC?

9

SLOW PRACTICES AND STORIES

Introduction

This chapter on slow practices and stories is an opportunity to bring examples from the early childhood educators and teacher educators in my study, who are working in different 'timefull' ways with stories. These include techniques that are very well documented to lesser-known approaches in a range of ECEC contexts. This can only be a brief introduction to thinking about literacy practices through a temporal lens but is intended as a springboard for discussion.

I was first challenged to think about this theme in a conversation with Mari Pettersvold, one of my Norwegian colleagues. Mari's question: 'How to be slow with a book?' has remained with me and has been one of the catalysts for my research. The juxtaposition of the word 'slow' and 'book' took me by surprise. It resonated with Honoré's desire as a parent for the 'one-minute bedtime story' (Honoré 2004: 2) that we saw in Chapter 1. This idea encapsulated the complete opposite of Mari's question, when Honoré found himself considering how to be *as quick as possible* at reading a story. I am hearing an echo from my own distant parenting experience of a small voice saying 'Again, again'. . . . asking for a story to be repeated once more as I attempted to creep out of their room.

Revisiting a text can be one way for young children being able to enjoy a book slowly, over time. Several of the examples that emerged from my interviews referred to this revisiting or repeating stories in different ways. So, it will be this connection between slow practices and revisiting that will feature in each of the examples in this chapter, together with the importance of the relational and contextual in young children's immersion in stories and storytelling. The *relational* emphasises the importance of the social aspects of engagements with stories that have the opportunity to grow over time. The *contextual* highlights the importance of young children recognising themselves and their lives and histories in the stories

DOI: 10.4324/9781003051626-11

that unfold. There is a wide gulf between the slow practices with stories that we will look at here and the focus on literacy skills that young children may encounter in ECEC in some contexts. The emphasis on disembodied phonics taught to the test for children in reception classes in England is one stark example of how far removed immersion in shared stories can be for some young children.

Malaguzzi drew attention to the inherent enjoyment in this slow practice with children:

> There is the pleasure of repetition that the child pursues through long repetition and is an acquired competency children can only let go at a later point when they start to realise they are acquiring many competencies that they can abandon this one. Repetition is a pleasurable game for children. Just think how many times children love to be told the same tales, the same stories, using the same words and the same situations. This need is part of the child.
>
> *(Cagliari et al. 2016)*

Being confident to explore stories slowly with young children does not necessarily come naturally. This chapter includes an example of an approach developed by Clodie Tal and colleagues in teacher education in Israel that has explored how to support ECEC students to develop these skills.

I'm going to begin by a way of listening to young children's own stories unfold.

Developing slow knowledge with Helicopter Stories

One of the books that I have faithfully kept with me since my teacher training in the early 1980s is *Wally's Stories: conversations in the kindergarten* by the American educator Vivian Gussin Paley, first published in 1981. The title of the book in red type on the spine of my copy has almost faded away but the children's stories from their year in kindergarten and Paley's skill in enabling the stories to be told and acted out by the children in an atmosphere of shared interest and respect, has stayed with me. Paley's work is the inspiration behind the Helicopter Stories technique of storytelling and story acting, developed in the UK by Trisha Lee (Lee 2015, 2022; Flewitt et al. 2017) – my first example of developing slow practices with stories. The title for the technique is taken from 'The boy who would be a helicopter' (Paley 1990). I turn to one of my study participants, William Clark, a teacher in Inner London to explain further:

> So particularly during my time in early years, I was a big proponent of the Helicopter Stories approach so, based on the teachings of Vivian Gussein Paley as adapted by Trisha Lee and Makebelieve Arts. It is an approach which is a storytelling and story acting approach. The idea being that you listen to children tell the stories you don't correct, you record the words exactly as they say them on an A5 piece of paper. They choose a character that they

might want to perform as and then at the end of the day they perform it with their peers, so they get to see their ideas become real. And it has some very nice processes within it around it being democratic so [the child who is the storyteller] chooses their character but everything else is offered around the circle or on the stage. And that's, I think, has a nice element of inclusiveness to it.

(William Clark, interview, October 2020)

So there are the two elements of the story: its telling by the author and then the second stage of story acting. There is a strong temporal element to this approach that involves listening on many levels by educators and children and then revisiting as the story is acted out together with the possibility of returning to the story over an extended period of time.

It definitely takes time. You can't rush it because you have to take the time to go to the children and to listen. And then you need to have the time to act the story out. In terms of evidence, if you were thinking about it in terms of quick, fast, regular evidence, it wouldn't work. You couldn't say 'we expect a story from every child once a week so that we can see the progress'. There just wouldn't be the time.

So in practice it's more a case of thinking: 'Over this year I'm going to have four, maybe five or six stories from this child and the stories are going to be spread out by a number of weeks because I want everyone to have enough turns'. But actually that's more meaningful because you get to really see their storytelling abilities change over those stories and that confidence change during those performances. And this informs your understanding of the child massively.

(William Clark)

We can see here the time commitment involved but also a deeper relationship with time over the course of a year where children are trusted to grow their stories and at the same time gain experience of speaking and acting together with their peers. This approach isn't designed for a quick fix tick sheet type of assessment. This can present problems within overpressured classrooms:

So, one of the challenges I think for Helicopter stories is the time commitment. So I looked at stories in a Year One context [five- to six-year-olds]. . . . And time is a real challenge. You have more space in Year One than you do in older primary school year groups, but it is still difficult . . .. How do we fit it in?

(William Clark)

Another counter point to a heavily measurement culture is the communal aspect of the Helicopter stories approach. Stories are developed by children and then shared and performed together. This collaborative, relational element can mean that it's building up a shared culture within a year group of children: 'a community of storytellers' (Flewitt et al. 2017: 38). This may be particularly valuable for children who are new to the group or who may be finding it harder to gain a sense of belonging due to their ethnicity or special needs. This slow form of storytelling and sharing may offer positive opportunities.

I explore this communal aspect of storytelling as a slow practice in the next example.

A slow unfolding of a story

There are several ways in which to answer the question 'How to be slow with a book?'

Stories offer the possibility to be enjoyed and expanded over weeks and months with young children. The discussion that follows describes an extended story project about *The Old Man and the Whale* by Stian Hole (2009) in a Norwegian kindergarten. The story centres on an old sailor and his brother who despite their animosity towards each other, rescue a whale. It is a story that has emotional depth. The author doesn't shy away from discussing complex feelings about being family. He does not patronise young children but treats them with respect. Children and educators each played significant roles in the development of ideas in this story project. This long extract from my interview with Mari Pettersvold, demonstrates how the story unfolded.

MARI: My favourite example is from some years ago (Pettersvold 2012) about project work with children for a whole year and it started with a book. And after six months, the ECEC teachers had planned to stop: 'Okay. We are finished. It's Summer'. But when the children came back in August they had a lot of questions. They had so much more to find out.

ALISON: What was the theme of the story?

MARI: It was about . . . different things but I think the main theme was about nature and taking care about nature and sustainability. It was a picture book for children . . .. They were working the way that ECEC teachers work. They were early childhood teachers in a good way. They created this from the inside. And they were, doing everything through dramatic episodes. And it was with 18 children, from three to five years old and we're using all the space and materiality and everything. Everything was about the project. All the walls and the furniture, and everything . . .. And it was quite complex. It was difficult for three-year-old girls and boys. But the way they were working, we can call it slow. I heard children, they were saying: 'Ah, now, I see'. So there were connections between everything. This project is still in my heart.

(Mari Pettersvold, interview, September 2020)

This comment, 'Ah, now I see' echoes Paley's description of her role as educator: 'The teacher must help the child see how one thing he knows relates to other things he knows' (1981: 213).

Mari continued:

MARI: It started in January in Norway in the snow outside with a suitcase. and in April this book about this man, an old man. They started to read a book about him. But then they made a new story. And that old man in the book . . . he needs some help to find a whale. [The title is] *The Old Man and the Whale* by the Norwegian writer Stian Hole and the title is a little bit Hemingway inspired.

ALISON: And the brothers if I remember rightly the brothers fall out, so there's the tension between them.

MARI: And some old love story and, things like that and it's quite interesting because in that book there's not a child at all. It's about those two brothers. So the teachers made the story that the whale was saved. The old man couldn't hear the whale sing anymore. So he had to start to find a way. And then he was going to take a plane from Northern Norway to Southern Norway with the suitcase and a lot of these things, and the history about how this could be outside in the kindergarten, in January in the snow. He went out of the plane in a storm. And then the teachers found a lot of the same things that are pictured in the book.

ALISON: So they actually brought objects in?

MARI: Yes, so, the children could follow the story . . . because the old man he has a cat. And so he asked the children, if they could look after the cat. He was trying to find a way. So they said Okay. And he also asked them if it was okay, to have some of his furniture in kindergarten because he was very old, and he needed to rest and they said okay. And in that way, all the things in the book were in the kindergarten, his pictures . . . coffee cup and his chair. And, yes, a lot of things. So after some months all those things, filled the room. And after the summer the children said we have to find his girlfriend.

ALISON: So that's interesting isn't it the teacher saying: 'Actually, no its finished, we've done that . . . for six months' and then the children even after the break, coming back and said: 'No, we need to do more . . .'

MARI: Yes, they gave the girlfriend. She hasn't a name in the book, but they called her Laura . . .. I think they knew that the old man who came back as a character was played by the teacher but they never mentioned it.

ALISON: No, it was understood.

MARI: They got letters to the kindergarten, from the old man, the playful way about that. I'm quite sure they knew that it wasn't from him.

ALISON: But it was one of those understandings between children and adults.

MARI: Absolutely. So it's quite magical. They got the letter. They had to sit down on the floor . . . That was one of the children's ideas. 'Sit down. We have got the letter' and they had to smell it . . . it was so silent as they passed it round and smelt it . . .. And they were also learning a lot of facts about whales at the same time, I think it was very inclusive too, some children will be good at it and interested and maybe some others not so. It had different possibilities. For me it's an example close to my heart because I saw also children experience how to be passionate about something. I think passion is quite important. And it's . . . interesting also because the teachers, they weren't waiting to see some interest from one or more children. They thought: 'Okay, we will do this but we need the children to be part of this'.

This is an example of a 'provocation' in Reggio terms that developed from a plan but remained open to how children would develop and extend the ideas. The excitement generated by the story filled the kindergarten and continued far longer than the teachers had anticipated and 'travelled' in unexpected directions. Children and educators were able to use their imagination. The extending of the story project beyond its intended length demonstrated the educators' openness to young children's agency over the timetable. The planned time to end the project was renegotiated. Multiple listening was evident throughout the project that resulted in sensitive and imaginative action.

There is a relational and inclusive aspect to this slow practice. The project created a common interest. It serves as another example of how sharing a narrative has the potential to include all children even if they are new to a group or to the country. It is not so dependent on a previous set of knowledge and experience but has the possibility to create new bonds, shared identity and shared memories. The importance of providing opportunities to create such a culture became apparent to me in Kris Kalkman's study of newly arrived migrant children's transitions within their early childhood provision in Norway (Kalkman and Clark 2017). One of the newly arrived girls was firmly told by some of the children 'Here we like playing princesses' as a way of stating what stories were permitted and as a result what narratives were excluded. Engaging in slow practices with stories with a whole class of children is not a guaranteed route to inclusion but offers possibilities.

Developing slow practices with stories may require practice for ECEC students. The third example in this chapter focuses on a specific programme for engaging with picture books in early childhood teacher education.

Revisiting stories over time

During a visit to a teacher education college in Tel Aviv, Israel I was introduced to the method of Repeated Picture Book Reading (Tal 2014; Tal and Segal-Drori 2015). Here I talked with teacher educators about their experience of working with students and in in-service training, to revisit stories, repeatedly, with small heterogeneous groups of children as a focus for listening and dialogue. One example of a student's experience of engaging over time with children about the picture book *Owl Babies* by Mark Waddell (1992) has stayed with me. In the story three owlets wake up to find that their mother has flown away. The siblings are anxious, particularly the youngest owlet. The siblings discuss what might have happened and then she returns to their tree. On reading and revisiting the story a group of children explained to the student teacher that the baby owls were waiting for their parents who had gone out to work but that they would come home. The children's own lives had found a connection with the picture book narrative and experiences had been shared.

During my interview with Clodie Tal she explained:

> In this context, it really is how to be focused and slow with a book, because really what teachers don't understand, and really what they're telling me is that the children will be bored, that's their fear. What they don't understand is when you observe, contemplate, discuss . . . in a group (and you don't need anything else, apart from the book and the people involved) . . . you read the book by yourself ten times, to understand what the book is about and then read it to your children. . . . You don't have to bring anything else. So it's both slow, and . . . about understanding the value of good books. Children are textual by their nature. You don't need anything more than the book, the children, and forget about the time.
>
> Students ask me technical things, 'Can I stop in the middle?' . . .. I don't care . . . as long as children are interested in it and they know at the end *what the book was about in their own world*. And it surprised me how many months it takes and that's another insight, you have to allow the adults the time also. Sometimes I'm impatient with adults and very patient with children! And I realised I had to also be patient with students, because it is a slow process to have them change their views because children lead us to a different place in time . . .. it takes students time to really incorporate in their own mind, this time of perception that really we are here for the wellbeing, learning, deep learning of the children. And you do all the core curricula you do it well when you're working in this way in this slow deep way with the children, and it doesn't matter if it's fiction, or if scientific books for children. You can use whatever text you want. But understand that it takes a while for children to contemplate. It is about the theory of mind. It takes a while for people to understand what something is about, and their minds make different connections than I make with them. I adopt this approach with my students, by really wanting to understand how they perceive things. How they perceive books, how they perceive whatever theories before I'm teaching them. And that's why my teaching is very slow. Really, it's very slow.
>
> (Clodie Tal, interview, September 2020)

I am struck by this phrase, finding out 'what the book was about in their own world'. This connects to two underlying pedagogical theories that underpin this programme. It is a 'life world approach' influenced by Max van Manen's phenomenological approach expressed as pedagogical thoughtfulness and tact (1991, 2016) (see Chapter 3) and draws on an ecological view of pedagogy, as Clodie and colleagues explain:

> We start by looking at the properties of the class as a living environment and the interrelationships among its components, rather than initially focusing on learning processes. We thus assume, based on an ecological view

of development and education, as presented for example by Bronfenbrenner (1979), that people are entities who move from one environment to another; they carry with them experiences, understandings, memories of contexts and ways of coping and isolated pieces of information. Furthermore, schools are important environments in which children and teachers live, relate, explore, learn and develop; however, their experiences in schools are embedded in their experiences in the world. Following van Manen's approach, we conclude that learning and teaching represent only one facet of the educational practice. Human relationships with and between children, among the teaching staff, and with the children's parents are perceived as a type of infrastructure of any preschool or kindergarten.

(Tal et al. 2008: 283–284)

Slowing down and revisiting picture book stories is one practice that can enable young children to connect the story with their own experiences of the world and for educators to listen and attend to these connections. What we are seeing here in the Repeated picturebook programme (RPBP) is an approach to story sharing that slows to enable experiential meaning to be shared.

Discussion

'Doing nothing'?

If a slower approach is taken to engaging with stories over an extended period of time, is there a danger of children being bored? This is one of the questions raised in this chapter. My response to this would be I think it depends to some extent on the active role of the educator through the process, skilfully listening for ways of engaging with children's current interests and experiences. Building on children's own storytelling and acting is one way of ensuring an active rather than a passive role for children, as we have seen in the Helicopter approach.

I return to a deeper question about slow practices, not limited to working with stories, that I first raised in Chapter 4 in relation to children as 'wayfarers' and the opportunity to 'go off track'. Does a slow pedagogy mean educators 'do nothing'? This thread is one that has emerged several times in my interviews. Clodie Tal points to this misconception as having been witnessed several decades earlier in Israel:

This is one of the misunderstandings of unhurried or unaccelerated pedagogy. And really, I witnessed in the 2000s when I worked with communities, three low socioeconomic communities, for two to three years. And we did in service training with a superintendent. And what I learned at those times, and in Israel at least the staff interpreted unaccelerated teaching as doing nothing, they had no idea about doing, they didn't do observations. It was hectic. So really, it's bad to work on skills and too heavily insisting on children learning letters but it's also bad to just do nothing. So it's more complicated than that.

(Clodie Tal, interview, September 2020)

It is more complicated. It is not a binary between hurry and acceleration and unhurry and inaction.

Hackett et al. (2020) express the skill involved in maintaining a quality of openness, in relation to engaging with children in museum and gallery spaces:

> This openness demands an ability to anticipate where children's interests lie, but at the same time to quickly respond to unexpected directions of thought, or 'lines of flight', that emerge in the moment.
>
> *(2020: 139)*

The attention to the potential of the moment echoes the focus of Mitchelmore et al. (2017) on the richness of everyday moments, discussed in Chapter 8. The word 'demands' conveys the forethought needed followed by a willingness and the energy necessary to run in an unexpected direction. These qualities connect with Froebel's concept of 'freedom with guidance'. This description above captures for me the intricate balance involved and shows how far such an approach is from 'doing nothing'.

Whose stories count?

I discussed in the introduction the importance of context for thinking about developing slow practices with stories and for young children to be able to make connections between their lives and histories. This raises questions about 'whose stories count?' whether the stories are spoken out loud or given time to appear as text, which story traditions appear on the bookshelves and which ethnicities and life experiences are illustrated and given status?

A slow pedagogy has the potential to be one in which time and space is made to pay attention to which stories are given visibility and value and to act to make positive change where children's worlds have not been represented. Clodie Tal in her interview emphasised that part of the importance of slow practices was not as an end point but as to what such practices have the potential to bring about in terms of social justice, children's rights and addressing inequality:

> What I have been saying before, is that these unhurried practices are the result, not the essence. So that's how I show them to students I don't want just to talk about unhurried practices, but I want to help them understand what's good education, what are the children's rights and I am very much worried about gaps between children who get at home good education and those who, if they don't get a good education preschool, which is unhurried but it needs to be meaningful. So that's why I'm talking about meaningful learning,

in depth learning more than unhurried education. Unhurried is one characteristic. But really, I'm talking about relationships, in depth learning, meaningful learning, reducing gaps between declarations and implementation.

(Clodie Tal, interview, September 2020)

Conclusion

This chapter has begun an exploration about what slow practices with stories can look like and who might benefit. We have seen how stories can provide different forms of 'stretched time' to be enjoyed together by adults and children. 'Being with' children as they explore stories in depth can enable new narratives to surface, beyond the first reading and listening. There has been a strong relational and potentially inclusive dimension to these approaches. The examples discussed have focused on ECEC educators and students and children. Such slow practices are not bounded by formal environments. Parents and other family members may discover other ways of 'being slow with a book' or exploring children's own stories over time in order to keep discovering what connections children make between the narratives they encounter and their own lives.

Questions

1 What do you see as the biggest pressures that challenge time for slow practices with stories?
2 How to be slow with a book? What can we learn from young children about this?
3 How would you avoid slowness becoming boring for children and educators?

10

SLOW LISTENING IN RESEARCH AND PRACTICE

Introduction

This chapter takes listening to young children in the context of research as a starting point and explores the intersection between listening, research, practice and time. The ideas discussed build on each of the earlier chapters, particularly on slow practices and pedagogical documentation (Chapter 7). This chapter gives space to different research methods and approaches that embody slow practices in research with young children and 'hold' time in particular ways: 'These ever changing stories and relations open the spaces of research for something new to emerge if we were to slow down and experiment with stories (data) that glow' (Millei and Rautio 2017). Examples of such slow encounters will include slow listening with video reflection and slow and deep listening to talk. I begin by looking through a temporal lens at some of the individual methods drawn together in the Mosaic approach.

Slow listening with the Mosaic approach

Finding different modes in which to listen to young children has been at the centre of my research since beginning the 'Voice of the child' study in 1999 with Peter Moss. This exploratory study resulted in the development of the Mosaic approach (Clark and Moss 2001, 2005; Clark 2017) and has led me, increasingly, to think about slow practices and slow knowledge.

> This multi-method, polyvocal approach brings together different perspectives in order to facilitate new understandings about young children's everyday lives. These insights can be constructed with individual children or with small groups in order to create both personal and shared narratives. The underlying values are based on an active and inclusive view of the child. The

DOI: 10.4324/9781003051626-12

research tools brought together in the Mosaic approach include a range of expressive arts-based languages in order to avoid reliance on verbal and written languages for listening to children's perspectives.

(Clark 2020: 138)

Slow practices are embedded in the Mosaic approach that is both multimethod and polyvocal. Working with multiple methods in one research approach requires a time commitment that is likely to exceed a single method strategy, especially if the one method, for example, is a quickly administered standard interview schedule. A polyvocal approach also represents an investment in time, as preparations need to be made for listening to a range of voices in appropriate ways. In addition to the multi-method and polyvocal elements, there are the opportunities for participants to frequently, and at various intervals of time, reengage with the documentation produced. This enables the Mosaic approach to have a slow and potentially deep relationship with time that may lead to the co-construction of slow knowledge, as I first used this phrase in 2010:

> Participatory, visual research methods provide the possibilities for young children and adults to engage in alternative forms of knowledge construction that in turn present challenges to researchers and research audiences. These complex explorations do not provide quick solutions to 'user engagement' but may contribute to new understandings between children and adults, professionals and lay communities. Perhaps this can be seen as a form of 'slow knowledge' not retrievable in the same way through a questionnaire but with the possibility of more rewarding and surprising results.
>
> *(Clark 2010b: 122, quoted in Clark 2017: 154)*

This next section looks briefly at how some of the individual methods included in the Mosaic approach may be understood as slow practices that provide opportunities for the co-construction of slow knowledge.

Stopping to observe

Research with the Mosaic approach starts with a narrative form of observation, as a way of laying a foundation for the other ways of listening to children that follow: a narrative form of observation was chosen to complement the other tools in the Mosaic approach, adapted from the use of narrative accounts or 'Nursery Stories,' devised by Peter Elfer and Dorothy Selleck during their three year study of under-threes in day care (Elfer and Selleck 1999 in Clark and Moss 2001: 35). Narrative observations slow to the pace of the child and seek to record the smallest details of their lives, in real time as episodes unfold. This element of the Mosaic approach is of particular importance when listening to and observing the youngest children in ECEC and children with special needs. A key part of listening to young children is observation and this involves a decision to give full attention to what is happening and so to be fully present in the moment. It is difficult to observe without slowing to the pace of the child or children you are observing. Such a decision to adopt the slow practice of observation involves a conscious relationship with time. The type of observation chosen will influence the rhythm of the relationship between observer and observed.

Slowing down and speeding up

Building on observations, another potentially slow practice incorporated into the Mosaic approach is a child-led tour. Here the adult adjusts their speed to the pace of the child as a way of listening. Young children are asked to show the adult researcher around an environment and for the children to document what is 'important', by talking about the places and taking photographs or drawing. The guided aspect of the tour means that the adult is not in charge of the pace at which this research activity happens. Children may come to a halt, for example, to examine a significant tree or speed up to catch a friend who is passing by. The original idea was adapted from a technique used in International Development to listen to local people about their area:

> Transect walks (Hart 1997), used in participatory Rural Appraisal is a method of gathering detailed information about an environment from the people who live there: 'systematically walking with local guides and analysts through an area, observing, asking, listening, discussing, learning.
>
> *(Clark and Moss 2001: 27)*

Here is an example from my third study, Living Spaces, a longitudinal study with children aged three to eight years in the re-design of their early childhood education environment (Clark 2010a):

> Jules took me on a tour of the nursery with one of his peers, Helen who was also four years old. The children were in charge of taking photographs to record the walk. This time Jules used a digital camera and reviewed his photographs as they were taken. I took notes of where we stopped on the tour, using a 'stepping stone' template to help me document the places in each photograph and the comments made . . . . This was a quick running record which needed to keep pace with the swift speed with which the children carried out the tour. Helen and Jules also carried a digital recorder, which enabled a transcript to be made of the conversations. The tour lasted fifteen minutes.
>
> *(Clark 2010a: 58)*

There is something special that can happen when walking and talking with young children but it is not necessarily part of everyday ECEC practice. It can be one of the 'in between' moments where conversations happen and relationships can deepen. Emma Dyer commented on the value of walking and talking with children in her role as a Reading Recovery teacher in a primary school, with six-year-olds (see Chapter 5):

> I had a little tiny room, which was at the top of the school, it was an old Edwardian school building. And the children who I was working with were out in a portacabin in the playground. And so actually, not only did I spend time teaching [the children in the programme], but it would probably take five or ten minutes to get them out of the classroom and walk them around. And so that was quite a big part of it, you know, that conversation with them as we went to the room. We might take a little detour and go a different way or, I don't know, just kind of settle them in. And so I think that was another aspect of it. That was a slow practice.
>
> *(Emma Dyer, interview, June 2020)*

Walking can also be a form of research enquiry in a/r/tography, a methodology that brings together the practices of artmaking, researching and teaching/learning within the arts and education (Irwin 2013). This bringing together of roles blurs the distinction between artist, researcher and teacher (Rajabali 2022). There is an inherent slowing down to a shared rhythm when walking is involved in this way (Triggs et al. 2014).

Slowing down to talk

Conversations between researchers or educators and young children can occur through several of the individual methods in the Mosaic approach, such as the child-led tour or map-making. However, it seemed important to create an opportunity for children to take part in a short interview about the research topic in question. So in my second study, Spaces to Play (Clark and Moss 2005; Clark 2017), researching changes to an outdoor play area with young children and educators; the focus of the interview was about children's views and experiences of the current environment and their opinions about how it could be improved. There is a slowing down to the pace of the child or group of children required and the adult tries to pay full attention to children's talk. We will explore another form of listening to talk – conversation analysis – later in this chapter.

Slowing down with visual images over time

Working with young children's visual images, whether photographs or drawing, has been an important multimodal element of developing the Mosaic approach (Clark 2011, 2014). It has been one of the ways to 'slow down the adult journey to deciding on meanings' as Cook and Hess (2007: 42) describe. The geographer Gillian Rose (2016) identifies four sites in a critical visual methodology: the production of the image; the image itself; the circulation and the 'audiencing' (2016: 24–47). So in working with the Mosaic approach there can be a slowing down involved firstly in accompanying the taking of the image (or as we have seen a speeding up). But something else is happening with time in the taking of the image. Lena Magnusson (2018) in her research with young children's photography in ECEC describes how time is dissolved in some way, there is a break with linear time. Magnusson continues by describing the camera as a 'memory maker'. Photography works in this way, regardless of the age of the photographer, but it is a very powerful tool in the hands of young children who have fewer other means of communication available for memory making. Working for example with Rees, one of the four-year-olds in the 'Spaces to Play' study (Clark and Moss 2005, Clark 2017), he expressed delight in taking his own photographs of the important markers for him in the outdoor play space. This joy in capturing each memory seemed particularly poignant, especially as Rees struggled to express himself with speech and language in the formal setting of the nursery.

This concept of children's photography as memory holders has been the focus of my more recent Norwegian study with Mari Pettersvold and Solveig Nordtømme, 'Children's photographic expressions' (Pettersvold and Nordtømme 2019; Clark 2019a). Working with children in their final year in kindergarten (five years old) we asked, 'What photographs would you like to take to remember the kindergarten?' There were several similarities between the themes that emerged about what was important for the children to remember in my earlier studies. This included attention to personal artefacts made by the children, close up images of friends and 'storied places' where favourite games were played. Karen Horsley has added further insights into young children's 'wise and intuitive photography' (Norris Webb 2014) in her study of how young children from a migrant background documented and celebrated their home lives through photography (Horsley 2022).

An important temporal dimension to working with the Mosaic approach is the multiple opportunities given to children and adults (Clark 2011) to revisit the documentation created, whether, for example, in books constructed of children's images or maps made by individual or groups of children of their photographs and drawings: 'The documentation . . . is then subject to review, reflection, discussion and interpretation by children and adults in a process of participant meaning making' (Moss 2010: xi). The time interval between creating and revisiting may be days, or weeks or even years, in the case of the Living Spaces study, a three-year study that included involving children in the planning and reviewing of learning environments. The visual documentation creates a platform for making revisiting possible in an accessible way.

My thinking about slow practices in research has been a long time in the making. When I began to write up the Living Spaces study I became increasingly drawn to the relationship between space and time (Bachelard 1994; de Certeau 1998). I chose 'temporal spaces' as the focus of one of the chapters (Clark 2010a: 116–130). One of the case studies I included in this chapter featured Samina, who I worked with for two phases of the study that were two years apart.

Samina was one of the children in the nursery class of the primary school. The class had been housed for several decades in a 'portacabin', a free-standing building not intended for long term use. The research followed the process of the building project to construct a new nursery within the school. Samina was one of the youngest four-year-olds and English was her additional language. When I first met Samina she appeared shy but interested in the camera that children involved in the research were using to take photographs of important things in their existing nursery. Samina was almost silent at the time in this learning environment. She joined in a tour of the nursery with one of the other girls and indicated that she would like to take some photographs in response to my question: 'Can you show me what's important here?' I was intrigued by one of Samina's photographs. She had included a large expanse of sky, edged by the school buildings and myself in a corner of the image. 'Is it about the sky?' I asked. Samina shook her head. I ventured another explanation, hesitantly: 'Is it about the aeroplane?' There was a tiny dot among the clouds. Aircraft frequently fly high over the school playground. Samina nodded so I added the caption 'the aeroplane' to the photograph in her photo book of the nursery that we were composing together.

When the new nursery was completed, two years later, I revisited the school and met Samina and her peers again. Samina, now six years-old, appeared very much at home in the school environment, talking away to me with her friends. She took part in another child-led tour to show me what was important to her. Much to my surprise Samina took another photograph of the sky and included this as one of her chosen images to discuss. We sat together and looked at my copy of her original photobook made during the first phase of the study, together with her new photographs:

SAMINA: What's that? That's you?
RESEARCHER: That's me. Yes, this is me, and it says . . . because there's something else in the picture, I don't know if you can see it, it's very small?
SAMINA: Aeroplane.
RESEARCHER: [Laughs] So two years ago you took a picture of an aeroplane and you took an aeroplane this time, as well, didn't you? I thought that was quite funny. So, I decided you maybe liked aeroplanes, but I don't know.
SAMINA: I . . . I love . . . home and I like . . . Bangladesh . . . country.
RESEARCHER: Oh right, yes, and that's your country and that's why you like aeroplanes. Ah, of course, that makes a lot of sense, yes.

(Clark and Flewitt 2020: 18)

Thinking again about this case study in the context of an article about competence and young children, Rosie Flewitt and I commented:

> The photographs were experienced as 'holding time', allowing Samina and the researcher to time travel back to earlier discussions. The images as material artefacts had 'power, vibrancy, timeliness [and] possibilities'

(Pacini-Ketchabaw et al. 2017, p. 6). Samina's strong sense of identity rooted in a distant place became apparent through this intra-action between people, materials, objects and place over time . . .. After two years in school in England, she continued to value her home in Bangladesh and her heritage culture as well as her home and her schooling in England. Samina demonstrated an ability to continue to hold these multiple identities together, finding traces in her urban British playground of her Bangladeshi roots.

(Clark and Flewitt 2020: 18–19)

Some research encounters have stayed with me over the years and these discussions with Samina continue to have an emotional impact. I think this is because Samina was able to demonstrate such competence through listening to her verbal and visual narratives. The extended period of time between my research visits provided an unusual temporal dimension to the relationship and highlighted how rare it would be within the English educational system for a six-year-old to be able to revisit 'work' made two years earlier and to have time to reflect on it herself and to talk about it with her peers and adults.

A slow pedagogy would take this longer view about children's learning journeys and include more opportunities for children to revisit and reflect on earlier narratives (see Chapter 11).

The first part of this chapter has set out to examine the Mosaic approach through a temporal lens. I now turn to examples from my interviews about different ways of slow listening and revisiting with young children, educators and early childhood students in research and practice, that expand on some of the forms of listening I have raised.

Slow listening with video reflection

Video reflection can be a powerful way of recording episodes of everyday life and returning to this 'real-time' footage to reflect (for example, Gillen and Cameron 2010; Powell et al. 2019). The technology involved enables moments in time to be paused and discussed, with the potential for this to enable 'multiple listening' (Rinaldi 2005, 2006) between those involved and other individuals. We heard earlier in Chapter 8 about the SOPHOS study, one of a number of cross-national studies that have drawn on a 'Day in the life' format of visual research building on Tobin and colleagues' video-cued ethnographic studies of preschool in three cultures (1989, 2009) that centre around the recording and discussing of video sequences of everyday life from multiple perspectives.

Kate Cowan explained to me the important role of video reflection in her study of digital documentation of young children's play with Rosie Flewitt (Flewitt and Cowan 2019; Cowan and Flewitt 2021). The study involved case studies of children between the ages of three and five in three diverse multicultural early years settings in London, including children who were encountering English as an additional language. Kate began by discussing the group of children they were most interested in studying:

> What we started out with was asking the teachers about which children in their classes seem to have [been the focus of the] most observations and which children had fewer observations and we used that to develop some case study children that we've looked at in each setting. But then quite interesting characteristics came out. So the children with most observations tended to be very confident, very loud, usually had English as a first language, would sort of seek adults out for attention and interaction, and were often engaged in . . . sedate indoor activities as a preference . . .. They're the star children. They're the ones that are really easy to do observations about. You notice them all the time. They come to you with learning gems. The children are bursting with these great examples. And so then we focused on the children who were the kind of opposite of that and who had fewer observations and . . . thinking about why that was the case. The characteristics of those children tended to be that they were quieter, described as being shy, often spoke English as an additional language or in early stages of learning English, who didn't seek out adult attention so much, and often chose to engage in quite a lively outdoor play. And they were described as being children that sort of 'flew under the radar'.
>
> *(Kate Cowan, interview, July 2020)*

I think this phrase, children who 'flew under the radar' is very telling. Liz Brooker in her book *Starting School: young children's learning cultures* (2002) focuses on young children whose cultural capital (Bourdieu 1997) sat at odds with the knowledge seen as appropriate in the reception classroom and who ran the risk of their skills and knowledge being unrecognised or invisible within the school context. Kate continues:

> So what we did was we focused on those children with fewer observations. They were the case study children in each setting and I invited the educators to use video to record episodes of their play, moments of their play. And then we watched them back together and . . . I've noticed looking back at some of the comments recently and there were quite a lot about time. So they said things like, 'It slows down your thinking'; 'The time, you have the time to think a bit more deeply.' It's a more holistic look, time to consider more things.' 'You can see it in a different way when you look later.' And I think you see more when you're watching it back.' So, there seems to be the sense that actually, they felt that the video was helping them to look more slowly and carefully and then actually see the children differently.
>
> *(Kate Cowan)*

Here we can see an example of how setting aside time to watch the video of the play episodes became a valued slow practice. The comments suggest that engaging with the video slowed down the educators' thinking processes. Christina MacRae has explored this dimension of video reflection further by investigating episodes in slow motion (MacRae 2019). Here digital technology has opened up new avenues for slow practice.

Kate continues by discussing how video reflection lends itself to multimodal analysis that pays attention to a range of modes of communication, and is not limited to the spoken word:

> So had a few examples where I thought that that little girl was just standing at the back and was really disengaged but actually now I'm watching I can see that she's watching her friend and then when her friend does it she joins in so she's copying her friend, and that sort of thing. So those snap interpretations that you make in a moment, the teachers were going back and questioning them and revisiting them through the use of the video. It seems to be a helpful tool for slowing down attention to the moments that might easily be overlooked in a busy classroom. And I think video is interesting, particularly because it's this multimodal record. I'm interested in the difference between what can you capture on a post-it note when you're doing an in the moment observation snapshot (which by its definition by the metaphor is very quick, one moment: 'got it'), in comparison with something that is actually a little bit more time consuming but enables you to capture some of the movement, gesture, facial expression those kind of subtle parts of children's play and learning that may be harder to describe in words. So, I think, I would argue that video was in that instance a more democratic and equitable way of looking and listening, and a way of . . . trying to value all children's signs of learning rather than the star children that may be able to demonstrate their learning in particular ways.

Kate contrasts the type of details that are possible with an 'observation snapshot' recorded on a post-it note to the more in-depth observation that is possible through returning to episodes, watching and pausing video recordings. But the main challenge of regularly adopting a slower form of observation and reflection is the need to prioritise the time involved. Kate describes some of the strategies that educators in her study adopted to face this challenge:

> But the challenge of this is that it was finding the time to watch it back so we did it as part of the research. And the schools were really generous with taking the time to do that with me but you know we did acknowledge that it would be tricky to do that regularly with large quantities of video. So they were kind of themselves developing strategies for that so someone in one school they were saying that well I think we would use it for the children that are flying under the radar so we would, if there were particular children who we were, trying to understand a bit more than we might use

it purposefully for them . . .. So they were coming up with sort of solutions about ways to use it, not all the time but purposefully for looking at particular types of play or particular children to kind of try and foster that like slower looking.

(Kate Cowan, interview, July 2020)

The use of video or still photography as tools for slow listening can 'disrupt' the present moment. Each raise ethical questions. These include who is in charge of the camera or in the viewfinder? Who selects or edits what is understood as important? Who is the audience for the images, how are they viewed and where are they stored (Rose 2016; Clark 2014)?

Slow and deep listening to talk

The final two examples in this chapter bring listening to children's talk centre stage. The first is about working with 'conversation analysis' (Bateman 2015). The second is a discussion about Pedagogy-in-Participation (Formosinho and Oliveira-Formosinho 2008, 2016; Oliveira-Formosinho and de Sousa 2019) that places listening in depth to young children at the centre of practice. This builds on my earlier discussion (Chapter 4) about the opportunities for 'diving deep' in a slow pedagogy and about pedagogical documentation (Chapter 7).

We begin with Amanda Bateman's account of how she uses conversation analysis with her ECEC students in New Zealand to teach this slow way of listening and awareness:

> I think one of the things that teachers often do is they 'do teaching'. And so they go in and they talk about things immediately . . .. This is where the usefulness of conversation analysis comes in where you see your audience or your recipients as the 'conversation recipient', their level of knowledge and you shape your talk to fit their knowledge and understanding. So, for example, I would talk to you about early childhood concepts because I know that you know. My husband and I would talk about them in a different way. You are always altering your talk to recipients. And so, in teacher pedagogy I think that conversation analysis is quite key because you wouldn't just go in and teach and talk about something because the children might already know about that thing.
>
> *(Amanda Bateman, interview, September 2020)*

This starting point of attuning your talk to your conversation recipient requires an ability to take your time to find out what your conversation partner already knows. Emma Dyer mentioned a similar principle about the first two weeks of the Reading Recovery programme (see earlier in this chapter) that focused on 'roaming round the known'.

Amanda designed a reflective practice assignment for her ECEC undergraduate students to carry out during their second-year placement or practicum:

> I've asked the students to go out, make a recording of an interaction that they have with a child . . . for one to three minutes, so quite a brief interaction. I suggested then that they took an object with them or they talked about an object that the child was interested in as it's useful to have something to talk about. Record that interaction either audio or video, and if they were younger children, we really push to try and get that video recording, because gesture obviously is really important. Then go back and transcribe the recording using conversation analysis transcription conventions. We did a little bit of conversation analysis practice in class. I explained to the students that they were not going to be marked on your rigour of conversation analysis and transcription symbols. My advice was to just make a note of the turn taking sequences, if there were long or short pauses and to just analyse that in terms of what the child has said and how they responded to that child and to bring this together with the literature around pedagogical interactions. So the written assignment was divided into: 'What did we talk about? How did we talk about it?' followed by a detailed reflective section at the end: 'What would I do differently in my future practice?' When the students did this assignment they always said: 'I didn't realise I talked so much!' or 'I completely didn't listen to the child then I took it off in a completely different direction!' All of these things. Every year they used to say: 'If you'd have told me, if you had transcribed it and you'd have given me feedback saying you needed to do this I wouldn't have listened, but because I've had to look at it myself and analyse my own practice' . . . that works really well.

This active involvement of the students in the process seemed to be a crucial part of the learning process. Amanda continued:

> They had to do it themselves and reflect on their own practice. . . . That was a good example I think of how you can make students aware of how slow and how deep these interactions should be with children, and how you yourself as an educator offer facilitation so that every time you have an interaction with a child, not only in university but when you leave University, and have that knowledge with you to think about, to reflect on how you interact, how you talk with children was really useful.
>
> *(Amanda Bateman)*

Working with conversation analysis in this way in early childhood teacher education is an active process that demonstrates the value of slowing down to listening intently not only to what children are saying but to how as educators the questions, phrases and gestures we use can have a profound impact on how children are able to respond.

I have chosen one final illustration of slow and deep listening that emerged from my interviews as it describes an approach embedded in practice:

> Pedagogy-in-Participation is a pedagogy of holistic and integral nature focused on making real children's rights in the day-to-day pedagogic development through the development of an educational intentionality that attunes children and educators' participation in co-constructing learning journeys.
>
> *(Oliveira-Formosinho and de Sousa 2019: 35)*

Júlia Oliveira-Formosinho discussed with me the emphasis on listening to every child in this model of a participatory pedagogy she developed with João Formosinho working in a Portuguese context, and how such an approach relates to slow practices:

JÚLIA: Even looking back to history, it looks like the understanding of the slow practices are connected with participatory pedagogies that really want children to be included, to have a voice. And it takes time to give voice, it takes time to document voice, it takes time to negotiate the inclusion of voice. For instance, I've been following some professionals that I think do it very well, and sitting down with the children, listening to how they do it. The educators ask the children on a Friday: 'Are we happy with our week? What do we dream for next week? What compromises do we want to celebrate? How are we going to go about the same?' and so on. All that is a process that takes time.

ALISON: When you say 'compromises' can you just say a bit more about that?

JÚLIA: Oh yes, because in Pedagogy-in-Participation we have these talks. They have a lot of sitting down and conversations we like them to enjoy the work first. We draw attention to pedagogy just being about conversations, shared conversations collaborative conversations about life and learning and so on. So don't be too concerned with techniques. Enjoy the pleasure of having a conversation with one of your children, the group as a whole, small groups and so on. And 'feel' what's there. What's the ethos of the group at the moment? and try to make a compromise between the curriculum, the national guidelines and the dreams, the plans the willingness, the desires of the children. So, don't go one way or another, try to compromise between the two.

JÚLIA: Knowledge requires conversation, normal conversations, human conversations. Of course, it requires knowledge but is it . . . just techniques or is it about just being together and listening to each other and having conversations with each other? So this is very needed for my understanding of slow knowledge. Yes, of course it is necessary. The game between individualization and individual life individualised hopes and dreams and collective hopes and

> dreams . . . The quick fix type of curriculum is very 'efficient' when work-
> ing with the collective. It's a recipe for the total classroom, but participatory
> pedagogies need to go between individualising and listening to the group
> and listening to the collective and to the groups and to the individual. It's a
> constant, constant movement between individuals, groups to collective events.
>
> *(Júlia Oliveira-Formosinho, interview, October 2020)*

This is a pedagogy that is rooted in the relational and is a dynamic process, moving
between individual children, groups and the wider community of children and
adults. I am struck by the honesty and pragmatism at the heart of this approach.
The questions to children: 'Are we happy with our week?' as part of a conversation to review experiences shared and 'What do we dream for next week?' show
participation in action but this listening is also realistic about the constraints,
the compromises made as a learning community: 'trying to make a compromise
between the curriculum, the national guidelines and the dreams, the plans, the
willingness, the desires of the children. So don't go one way or another, try to
compromise between the two.' Such compromise may apply to slow pedagogies
in many contexts.

Discussion

'Was being, am being, will be'

The intersection between listening, research and time in ECEC is related to the
relationship between the adults and children involved. I have had the rare privilege
of being involved as a researcher in a funded longitudinal study with young children (Clark 2010a). This placed an unusual temporal dimension to the relationships I formed with the children that included intense periods of daily interaction
as they co-constructed with me their views about their existing learning environment and then returning after more than a year to listen again to their views and
experiences and to revisit their earlier thoughts. This fragmented, longitudinal
relationship with a group of young children at different stages of their life in nursery and school is in contrast to the everyday engagement between educators and
the children in their group, class or year group. There is one similarity, however,
between the adults involved whether in a longitudinal or everyday role – how
do we view the children we are engaging with? This has a profound impact on
what we think children are capable of and how they can participate. Beth Cross
has applied some of these questions in a study concerning the phenomenology of
participation drawing on the work of Bakhtin (1981) and Gadamer (1975). Cross's
study focused on older children engaged in the transition between primary and
secondary school. Focusing on the dialogue between adults and children she makes
the case for the importance of 'relational temporality'. Cross extends Uprichard's
(2008) construct of children as beings and becomings to make explicit the lived
experience that both children and adults bring to their day to day relationships.

She refers to three temporal stances: children as beings, becomings and 'having been'. She asks:

> Do we allow ourselves to be in the moment (human being)? Do we share a sense of what we have yet to learn or become (human becoming)? How do we convey prior experience or balance that with the present (human having been)? How do we recognise and respond to young people's own stances, past, present and becoming? Do we give enough importance to young peoples' past experience and their interpretive use of it? These questions are all ones of relational temporality. They have to do with how we experience and identify ourselves within the passage of time and how we assess others within the flow of time. The considerations above funnel into the primary analytical question: How does a sense of temporality inform practitioners' sense of their project with children?
>
> *(Cross 2011: 31)*

These questions also pose a challenge to dialogue between adults and children in ECEC, for example, 'Do we give enough importance to young children's past experience and how they draw on this prior knowledge?' Some of the methods discussed in this chapter provide possible ways to begin to do so but 'giving importance to' emphasises the need to go beyond 'techniques' or 'tools' for listening to consider what status is given to such lived experience and what changes may result? Taking another of Cross's questions and reapplying it to an ECEC context: 'How do we experience and identify ourselves within the passage of time and how do we assess others within the flow of time?' I understand this to highlight how our own sense of self, our personal histories and hopes for the future are involved in how we engage with young children and their abilities to participate. Questions of power and temporality are deeply connected, as Cross reminds us. Perhaps this raises the possibility of the term 'longitudinal' educators who are able to hold a sense of young children as 'was being, am being and will be' for whatever length of duration, short or long, the pedagogical relationship continues. We will return to these questions about the longer view in my next and final chapter.

Conclusion

Different timescapes have been explored in this chapter in relation to slow listening to young children in the context of research and practice. We have begun to look at how visual, participatory methods can contain a range of different timescales, within individual methods, in drawing methods together and in the returning to conversations and the artefacts made. The value of close attention to spoken and gestural interactions, as seen in the example of introducing ECEC students to conversation analysis, sits alongside the affordances of working with visual data. But the examples discussed in this chapter come alive through the relationships between children and adults, as researchers and educators. These relationships have a temporal dimension. These relationships are shaped by what we decide is of value in the present as well as how we view children's past, present and future. A further layer is added according to how we construct our own past, present and futures in the midst of research and practice.

Questions

1   In what ways can working with visual methods slow down adult assumptions about young children's priorities and interests?
2   How would you justify the time involved in using multimethod and multi-modal approaches to working with children's perspectives?
3   How might slow listening in research and practice increase the visibility of different groups of children?

PART 3
Moving forward

Part 3 considers what next? It acknowledges a discontentment with the status quo in terms of hurried education. The case is made for a 'timefull' approach to Early Childhood Education and Care (ECEC) that can offer a more sustainable and play-focused approach to early childhood across generations and communities.

Questions are raised about what a 'slow and patient' ECEC would look like? What are the challenges to slowing down and holding a longer view? Which groups of children might benefit most? This reconsidering of the relationship with time may in turn make it more possible to respond to the urgent issues for 21st century children, educators, parents and communities and the planet.

DOI: 10.4324/9781003051626-13

11
TIME FOR A RETHINK

Introduction

This final chapter returns to the link between thinking about time, practices and relationships and what is the purpose of early childhood education. Drawing on earlier chapters, I return to the concept of timefullness and the observation that 'the ways we experience, name and interpret time contribute to the kinds of communities we imagine and inhabit' (Badyer–Saye 2006: 96 in Swinton 2016: 63; see Chapter 3). A relationship with time is a given in education (Murris and Kohan 2021). This can include the limits of the school or nursery day, the schedules of parents and carers, the everyday routines that need to happen. This conversation is not about denying the importance of time but of working with time in a more conscious way, of being aware of what is enabled or is constrained by different approaches to time in ECEC and to make explicit what alternatives might be possible. I am emphasising talking about *time* as well as *slow*. I am suggesting that thinking about ways to be slow can be a way in but to then ask: what kinds of communities does slow enable? So, as in the example in Chapter 8, in slowing down mealtimes and rethinking how routines around snacks are arranged, what then becomes possible? It is more than the practices in isolation: what pedagogical transformations does this open up?

Timefull approach to ECEC

A timefull approach to ECEC may involve resonance and listening, resistance and making room for the longer view.

Resonance and listening

I return to the work of Hartmut Rosa here whose thinking about acceleration and escalation I discussed in Chapter 1 and the concept of resonance. Rosa does not see

DOI: 10.4324/9781003051626-14

slow as the answer to social acceleration but resonance. When discussing relationships in the classroom he sets out an ideal learning environment where:

> a web of resonance take shape in the classroom as a whole in which 'vibrating material' is negotiated and all present can participate. In this case focusing attention and responsive emotional involvement is essential and in this the teacher serves as an all but irreplaceable catalyst.
>
> *(2019: 246)*

This serves as an example in Rosa's argument of a resonant space. This image connects to a metaphor I have written about earlier (Clark 2010a) that I came across in Italo Calvino's monograph, *Invisible Cities*:

Invisible connections

I have been struck by the importance of the personal in institutional spaces for young children. Children have indicated through their photographs, conversations and map making how their immediate environment contains connections with people, objects and places which provide guides or way markers. These connections may be particularly intricate where a child has siblings in the school or setting, or where there are numerous objects or places which relate to themselves. The imaginary city, Ersilia, described by the Italian writer Italo Calvino, is one in which the invisible connections between people and places are made visible:

> In Ersilia, to establish the relationships that sustain the city's life, the inhabitants stretch strings from the corners of houses, white or black or grey or black-and-white according to whether they mark a relationship of blood, trade, authority, agency. When the strings become too numerous that they can no longer pass among them they leave: the houses are dismantled; only the strings and their supports remain.
>
> *(Calvino 1997: 76 in Clark 2010a: 80–81)*

I ended this reflection on invisible connections by posing the question: 'What would learning communities look like if these relationships were made visible?'

I am drawn to this image of the strings making connections visible. As a visual artist I have made installations with string including weaving a web around a building, following old nails and hooks left in the brick work. Working with this image of Calvino's to think about an early childhood environment there are some parallels. I encountered this in my first study developing the Mosaic approach. Gary, three years old at the time, took me on a tour of his nursery to show me what was important. He was quick to take me to the wing of the nursery that belonged to the youngest children. Here Gary took a photograph of his younger brother playing outside: 'the affectionate rapport they shared was apparent from their greeting' (Clark 2017: 62).

So some of the strings or invisible connections might be between children and siblings or friends. Other strings might represent hierarchies of authority or power among educators, parents and different groups of children depending on their status within the group. Strings to represent agency is an interesting one and would depend on the pedagogical culture as to how many agentic connections were visible. If this early childhood environment followed a participatory model where young children were enabled to exercise their agency frequently on a daily basis then the strings would be dense. However, a transmissive model might be seen to lead to fewer connections.

Rosa's 'web of resonance' emphasises the participatory element: 'Vibrating material is negotiated and all present can participate' (2019: 246). Resonance as a concept sets out to be inclusive rather than exclusive. Calvino's strings emphasise the visual but there is a stronger sense from Rosa's wires that these connections are 'alive', full of movement and sound. These vibrating wires represent communication. This for me is where listening fits into a discussion about the importance of resonance in a learning community and listening is a timefull practice.

Within Rosa's complex theory of resonance he identifies three different categories of resonant relationships on three axes: a horizontal dimension that includes resonant relationships with other human beings; diagonal resonance of resonant relationships with the material world and vertical resonance to the world as a whole, for example, through spirituality, art, nature or history (2019: 39–40). It is in the diagonal resonant relationships with the material world that Rosa includes an education environment where a responsive relationship is established between the subject matter and the learner. There is a connection, 'a segment of the world . . . "speaks"' (p. 40).

Rosa contrasts resonant relationships with muted relationships. One interpretation of a muted relationship is one where listening is all but absent whereas unmuting or finding connection makes listening possible. A 'muted' early childhood culture might be understood to be one in which there were fragile connections between children and adults and between the curriculum and children. This might be characterised by a solely transmissive model of learning where misunderstandings and assumptions about what views and experiences children bring to their exploration of the world are held.

Thinking about ECEC as a resonant space relates to the concept of the 'pedagogy of listening', as embodied in the preschools of Reggio Emilia (see Chapter 3 and 7). Carlina Rinaldi's explanation of the pedagogy of listening speaks to me of a resonant space that combines ideas about participation, agency, communication and relationship. She also brings us face to face with the question of time:

> Listening as time, the time of listening, a time that is outside chronological time – a time full of silences, of long pauses, an interior time. Interior listening, listening to ourselves, as a pause, a suspension, as an element that generates listening to others but, in turn, is generated by the listening that others give us.
>
> *(2006: 65)*

Listening in this way can be seen to not be dominated by clock time. Rinaldi's expression here: 'a time full of silences, of long pauses' helps add a further layer to understanding what a timefull approach to ECEC can look like. Rinaldi continues by discussing children's abilities with respect to listening and time:

> They possess the time of listening, which is not only time *for* listening but a time that is rarified, curious, suspended, generous – a time full of waiting and expectations. Children listen to life in all its shapes and colours, and they listen to others (adults and peers). They quickly perceive how the act of listening (observing, but touching, smelling, tasting, searching) is essential for communication. Children are biologically predisposed to communicate, to exist in relation, to live in relation.
>
> *(2006: 66)*

Gunilla Dahlberg and Peter Moss discuss in their introduction to Rinaldi's book, in this Contesting Early Childhood series, the ethical dimensions to such an intense form of listening:

> a pedagogy of listening means listening to thought – the ideas and theories, questions and answers, of children and adults; it means treating thought seriously and with respect; it means struggling to make meaning from what is said, without preconceived ideas of what is correct or appropriate. A pedagogy of listening treats knowledge as constructed, perspectival and provisional, not the transmission of a body of knowledge which makes the Other into the same.
>
> *(Dahlberg and Moss, in Rinaldi 2006: 15)*

The pedagogy of listening acknowledges the importance of doubt and uncertainty, of educators being comfortable with encountering difference and disagreement. There is a similar acknowledgement in Rosa's theory of resonance, where there is always the possibility of contradiction (2019: 344), of time for debate rather than an echo chamber.

Resistance

Reconsidering the relationship with time in ECEC is a political act. Malaguzzi indicated its importance in a speech he made at an international conference in Reggio Emilia in 1990 in the final years of his life:

> The question of time is a very strong question; it is enough on its own to overturn and revolutionise the lack of respect for time in pedagogy and schools. The right to play, to be idle, the right to work, in short a right that is as broad as possible.
>
> *(Malaguzzi, L. in Cagliari et al. 2016: 399)*

This study has shown that there are slow practices happening in ECEC that can be understood as a form of resistance against a clock-driven, accelerated and highly structured system. Nathan Archer has referred to such responses as 'micro-resistance': 'local, quiet, invisible but multiple' (2021). Drawing on situated critical pedagogies (McLaren 2005) McNair and Powell (2021) make the case for 'Froebelians as revolutionaries who are finding principled and creative solutions for educational resistance and reimaginings' (p. 1177).

MacRae et al. (2020) demonstrate what such reimaginings in relation to time can look like between museums and galleries and families with young children:

> The offer of safe-bases from which to venture from, of flexibility but, at the same time, of supple patterns and routines, all become political acts of inclusion, ensuring that time is allowed to flow at different speeds and intensities.
>
> *(2020: 140)*

Resistance is a multifaceted concept. A timefull approach to ECEC can be understood to involve resistance in different forms, at an individual level and in learning and caring relationships, to institutional and wider responses. The example given above about 'supple patterns and routines' connects with the slow practices discussed in Chapter 8 about the everyday where there is breathing space at times to adjust to children's rhythms. This is a form of resistance to the 'tyranny of the clock' (Rose and Whitty 2010; Pacini-Ketchabaw 2012). An emphasis on listening, as we have discussed throughout this book, can be seen as countercultural in some ECEC contexts: 'Being counter-cultural indicates a way of being that is against the flow' (Clark 2020: 136).

Here I want to return to Gert Biesta's ideas I referred to in Chapter 1 where he challenged the 'impatience' of schools. Biesta broadens the concept of resistance arguing that the experience of resistance is central to thinking about the purpose of education and the role of educators and children:

> Here we might say that the educational 'work' only really begins with the experience of resistance. It is after all only when children or students resist that they appear as subjects in the educational relationship rather than as (willing) objects of educational interventions.
>
> *(2012: 96)*

Biesta describes education as the connection between the child (or student of whatever age) and the world – placing this encounter in the middle ground between a child-centred approach and a subject-centred approach – in what he terms a world-centred approach. This creates an active role for the child and educator. Resistance, Biesta explains, is about establishing a dialogue, and unlike a contest, dialogue is understood as an ongoing process. He proposes that there are three possible next steps on encountering difference, an obstacle or something Other. If taken to extremes, these options can be firstly, to challenge until the obstacle is destroyed or secondly, retreating and hiding away or thirdly, to engage with what resists:

> The challenge for education therefore is to stay in (the) dialogue and to acknowledge that the difficulty of staying in this place is an essential dimension of what it means to engage *with* and exist *in* the world.
>
> *(2012: 96)*

This 'staying with' echoes Sylvia Kind's account in Chapter 4 of a slow pedagogy as 'being with' linking to the pedagogical approaches of Ted Aoki (Pinar and Irwin 2005; Lee et al. 2022) and van Manen (1991, 2016). Biesta refers to secondary school students working with resistant materials as one example of staying with:

> to establish a dialogical relationship between oneself and what is other – a process in which one will not only find out many things about the materials one is working with, but also about one's own ability to establish and maintain a dialogue, to work through the frustration, to work with the material rather than against it, and so on.
>
> *(2012: 98)*

A similar illustration could be given of young children engaging with materials in a studio space. Thinking with materials is helpful in order to grasp what such a dialogue can feel like but difference can be encountered in many ways, including for example in discussion, through stories and drama.

Biesta extends his argument about education further in a way that is most relevant for this book, by making the link between resistance and slow. As we saw in Chapter 1:

> All this suggests that the education of the will is a question of patience and perseverance, a process that needs time and attention. There is, in other words, no quick fix where it concerns the encounter with resistance and the ability to be 'in dialogue' with the world, with what is other and different.
>
> *(Biesta 2012: 98)*

The relationship between resistance and slow leads us to the concept of patience. I was at first wary of contemplating the relevance of this term in the context of ECEC. My initial reaction on reading and discussing Biesta's article brought associations between patience and passivity and submission. Patience is perhaps an unpopular word, at odds with the hurried culture discussed earlier. But patience can be a resilient, persistent, active, brave quality. There is room for this type of powerful patience in a timefull approach. I will return to this concept of patience shortly.

The longer view

I understand timefullness to be a layered and complex term that encompasses taking the longer view about the purpose of education, about educators' role, children's past and future. This is paired with a longsighted view about global concerns. Taking the longer view embodies an expansive relationship with time. Importance is given to the 'here and now', to deep attention to the present but in such a way that can encompass past and future: a '*here and now and*' approach.

I suggest that avoiding short termism and standing up for taking the longer view is a priority for education at this moment in history and for our planet. My experience as an educator who began teaching in the mid 1980s in England, followed by several decades in educational research, is that education policy has often been forgetful or dismissive of the past and prone to reinvention. The circular debates about what is quality is a case in point. Taking the longer view in ECEC includes being mindful of early childhood traditions, such as Froebelian practice and continuing to explore its relevance today (for example, Bruce 2020; Tovey 2017; Bruce et al. 2020). This links to ideas I discussed in Chapter 4 about the importance of slow knowledge as expressed by the environmentalist David Orr. One phrase in particular seems important to restate here: 'Fast knowledge is always new; slow knowledge often is very old' (1996: x).

Longer term thinking can appear countercultural, particularly if set against the backdrop of instant communication and hurry. There is more attention being given to the dangers of short-termism particularly in relation to the climate crisis and from those whose disciplinary perspectives lead them to stretching their thinking across centuries and millennia. As I discussed earlier (Chapter 3), I came across the concept of timefullness from two very different directions, one from theology and one from geology. These are both disciplines that take the longer view.

Challenging short termism can also apply to thinking about how young children's past, present and future are approached. A 'here and now and' viewpoint could be one in which the present moment is not completely overshadowed by either narratives relating to children's past or their predicted future but where each temporal dimension is acknowledged and valued. This builds on Cross's construct of 'relational temporality' (2011) discussed in Chapter 10.

Focusing first on the 'here and now': 'Do we allow ourselves to be in the moment?' We have seen many examples throughout this book of where pursuing slow practices, whether, for example, outdoors, with materials, in everyday routines or with stories can immerse children and educators in the present.

But there is also the temporal dimension in ECEC of viewing children as human becomings. This can become the dominant focus, driving children towards prescriptive outcomes but also can be approached with openness, mindful of each child's unique potential. The third temporal stance that Cross outlines makes explicit each child's past. So, taking an expansive view of time in ECEC can be understood as one in which children are viewed as beings whose previous views and experiences are recognised, however short that past might be as well as future becomings. Reexamining relationship with time stretches beyond questions of pace and tempo and timetables. It involves the valuing of the past in the present as well as into the future and slow knowledge in turn can contain this recent past knowledge that young children hold. Taking the longer view as part of a timefull approach to ECEC acknowledges the value of being able to look forward and back with young children and their families.

I have outlined some key qualities of a timefull approach to ECEC that includes the concepts of *resonance, resistance and listening, patience* and the *longer view*. Drawing these ideas together I propose that a counterpoint to the hurried, future-driven, outcome focused ECEC is a *patient kindergarten* that embodies slow pedagogies and values slow knowledge. (I am using the term *kindergarten* here as shorthand for talking about ECEC in its many and diverse forms including family day care.) As I have discussed in this chapter the term patience draws on Biesta's caution about the impatience of society towards education and points to a reasserting of alternative narratives for early childhood.

A patient kindergarten that embodies slow pedagogies and values slow knowledge could:

- Make time, place and materials for children to explore what they think through play
- Create opportunities to deepen and extend children's learning through 'being with' and revisiting moments through pedagogical documentation
- Make time to listen to children's ideas and experiences through a range of expressive languages
- Prioritise time to listen to multiple perspectives from families and colleagues
- Be a place of resistance, unafraid to encounter uncertainty and difference and to challenge policies that sit uncomfortably with pedagogical principles
- Be a place where taking the longer view is valued: about children's lives, about education and the planet
- Value the 'here and now and': pay close attention to the present whilst recognising children's past knowledge and experiences and being mindful of their future

Challenges to a timefull approach to ECEC

There are many potential challenges to be addressed in reexamining the relationship with time in ECEC and will be influenced by the political, cultural and policy frameworks in each context. As discussed in Chapter 1, a discourse of measurement can distort what is seen as of value for young children and can mitigate against periods of 'unfragmented time'. We have seen how education policies that emphasise 'school readiness' in the early years can be understood as taking a proleptic view of time (Jewitt and Jones 2005) that allows the future to overshadow the importance of the present moment.

There are some common obstacles that relate to processes of reimaging dominant discourses and there are historical precedents for *supporting* such changes, as Peter Moss discussed:

> I think if we are going to move towards slow pedagogy my sense is that its enormously more rewarding but that its more complex too and so often what has happened in the past is when people have introduced exciting new ideas the kind of necessary support has not been in place hence a lot of examples of progressive education seem to last only a very short time because they depend on charismatic leaders or a particular combination of events . . .
>
> One of the really important things about Reggio Emilia is their great attention to conditions and supportive systems. What they have wanted to explore one might say is slow pedagogy but what they have said is 'What do we have to do to enable this?' And then they set in place, all sorts of things, pedagogistas, atelieristas, the teachers working in pairs so the approach is rooted in deep practicality and in a way is scrapping all the performativity pressures. It's replacing those with other forms of curriculum assessment, it's about putting support in place. It's about reconceptualising education and educators, this change of identity and subjectivity so that people will think of themselves in different ways as people working not in a factory or a business but in a public service so all of those things in terms of governance, identity and subjectivity need to be addressed.
>
> *(Peter Moss, interview, May 2020)*

I want to emphasise here the need for a deep practicality and collaborative support to promote a less hurried, more timefull approach to ECEC. The debate about the relationship with time raised in this book is not intended to add further pressures to individual educators. This has been a discussion that adds to other insistent voices that call into question an epistemology based on the quickly acquired, scripted and easy to measure (Holt 2002; Biesta 2012, 2013; Ball 2016; Atkinson 2011, 2015; McNair et al. 2021; Robert-Holmes and Moss 2021). The aim is to offer a different way of articulating alternatives and to start with the small moments.

One challenge raised in my interviews was how to *communicate* these ideas to parents, as Tahmina Shayan commented:

> The challenge is being judged. The challenge could be that parents might say, 'Oh, why didn't you do this at this time?' And you are again being questioned by parents, but also it'd be nice if you can have a chat with families and say this is what you're trying to do and for this reason because you're feeling that children are being so rushed daily that they have no time to be, and children are also stressed, even very young children can be stressed out . . .
>
> And I think it would be best to communicate that with families and educators and tell them what it is that you're trying to do and why. And then

maybe creating spaces where children and educators and families can come together to do something that you're really enjoying . . . and you're having a cup of tea together and everyone's taking time sharing stories and nobody's rushed. Comparing those moments with . . . 'Now you've got 30 minutes and this is what you do . . .'

(Tahmina Shayan, interview, November 2020)

And communicating ideas also relates to the specific language employed. Is the phrase *slow practices* helpful or are *unhurried* or *timefull* terms more understandable?

What do we mean by slow pedagogy? The word *slow* doesn't capture the richness of slow pedagogy. It doesn't invite parents and families to think about what are the children going to do here? Are they going to play slowly?

(Tahmina Shayan)

I am aware that there is a historical legacy to the term 'slow' in relation to education in some contexts, including the UK where 'slow learners' has been used in the past as a derogatory phrase to refer to children with learning disabilities. I don't think this should rule out the importance of thinking about slow but it does underline the need to communicate clearly this expansive approach to time.

The ability for educators to articulate pedagogical foundations is crucial here, beginning in teacher education. This in itself can be a complex process, involving patience and an openness to resistance in its many forms. The political and the personal are closely tied together in terms of transformative pedagogical change, as Kari Carlsen explained:

I think that has to do with different levels. We have talked about the political level. A change in the political level in the way I have to say they look at children's learning or how people learn things is necessary and there is beginning to be some discussion about this in Norway so change is necessary at a political level. And I think it has a lot to do with what teachers and staff in kindergarten think about what are their pedagogical foundations, their pedagogical landscape. How and to what extent are they aware of their own pedagogical platform? I think another key point is the organising of the day and the organising of the week. It's possible to organise, although you don't have a schedule for preschool (some do) but to be aware that you can organise the whole thing and have no time. You haven't the time to let children be in a sort of flow, to explore and build up their knowledge. If you organise so that the timeslots are short you are guaranteed not to reach these aims, this flow because 'you have to eat', 'now comes the fruit', 'Now we have to go out' . . .

(Kari Carlsen, interview, September 2020)

Again we can see how internal as well as external pressures can create stumbling blocks in the way of transforming practice. Other challenges may be inherent in seeking to take the longer view when working in systems that are wedded to short-term results. The journalist Richard Fisher identified obstacles or 'temporal stresses' to long term thinking, during his fellowship at MIT (Fisher 2020, 2023). He includes the habitual practices in organisations, the overload of technology that can focus on the immediate at the expense of wider perspectives and the impact of targets. To escape short-termism, Fisher argues 'we must reassess the targets by which we gauge success.' He concludes: 'If I've learnt anything about long-term thinking to date, it's that it is a collective and collaborative endeavour. . . . ' (Fisher 2020: n.p).

This leads me to the final section in this chapter to discuss, briefly, some of the possibilities for supporting a reimagined relationship with time in early childhood.

Possibilities

What I hope this book has shown are the many different forms of slow practices that exist in ECEC that offer alternatives to the image of the hurried child and hurried educators. This 'dictionary of possibilities' is not an exhaustive list. Dictionaries grow and definitions are debated, some fade and new meanings are added. I am aware of important languages that are part of such a dictionary of slow practices but are missing from this initial research. Three areas I would name here, among others, are firstly the infinite possibilities of engaging with music with young children in its myriad forms that can interrupt clocktime and introduce different rhythms and moods to ECEC (for example, Young and Ilari, 2019). Secondly, I would want to raise here the potential of digital play as a slow practice with innovative ways of 'being with' young children and across generations (for example, Cowan et al. 2021). Thirdly I draw attention to the wide body of indigenous knowledge that is embedded in local early childhood practices and can offer different possibilities for engaging with time with young children (Pacini-Ketchabaw and Montpetit 2019).

Co-constructing slow knowledge

We have seen, from the discussion earlier about challenges, the importance of finding ways to collaborate, exchange ideas and give and receive support in challenging dominant discourses. This emphasises how valuing and accumulating slow knowledge involves co-construction. There are many forms that such networks can take. These can be understood as 'communities of practice' or, as Peter Moss has described, a resistance movement offering possibilities of exploring alternative narratives to dominant discourses in ECEC. The relationship with time may be an implicit or explicit part of the dialogue. The 'common world' framework (Taylor and Giugni 2012; Common Worlds Research Collective 2019) is one example I have written about elsewhere (Clark 2020) that promotes a radical rethink about the relationships with place and the 'more-than-human' and exemplifies longer term thinking.

I have had contact with two different forms of collaborative, professional networks during this research.

The first is the London Refocus group, a study group of educators working with ideas inspired by the pre-schools in Reggio Emilia. This is one of a number of international, national, regional and local Reggio networks. London Refocus, like many professional groups, has had to adapt to being online over the past two years, due to the pandemic, but the pedagogical style of the group has remained one in which listening is central. 'Metaphors' is a recent example of the research focus of the group, where educators working in a range of early childhood provision and schools in the state and private sector meet regularly to share documentation and reflect on children's ideas and artefacts.

Pedagogical reflection, collaboration and support are characteristics of the Froebel network, that exists at an international, national, regional and local level. The Froebel Trust provides training, resources and research opportunities including a series of "Practitioner grants". Falkirk is one local authority in Scotland where there is a thriving Froebelian network, supported by early childhood pedagogues, that connects educators locally and nationally (McNair and Powell 2021: 1180). These examples illustrate collaborative approaches to challenging dominant discourses. There is a desire to do something different. There are both similarities and differences to these movements. I would suggest that 'timefullness' might be one of the common threads, a desire to value the present moment but also hold the longer view about individual children, about education and our planet; to make room to revisit ideas and to celebrate complexity. These are hopeful or perhaps hope-filled ideas.

Each of these networks are examples of how educators can increase their professional confidence together to, at times challenge the status quo, as Amanda Bateman explained:

> So, to be able to argue your case for what's best for children. So, like I was saying before if you are given policies or if somebody approaches you and questions your practice, you've got this 'kete[1]'of information, this knowledge, where you can argue your case: 'this is why I'm doing it like this. I can understand what you're saying but actually' and give them good experiences, good understanding of good practice that you can argue, I think, and that way you can stop this accelerated learning this pressure.
>
> *(Amanda Bateman, interview, September 2020)*

This chapter has set out to imagine what a timefull approach to ECEC can look like. I propose that this may involve resonance and listening, resistance and making room for the longer view.

This is not an easy path, particularly for those working within policy frameworks that support a hurried culture for young children and educators. But there are alternatives.

This book has sought to begin to bring together ideas that are perhaps dispersed at present. My desire is that this research may draw attention to where the slow practices are happening in ECEC practice and in teacher education to strengthen these alternative ways of working and to demonstrate how a different relationship with time is possible.

Conclusion

Finally, I return to the Slow Movement. Slowing down can be a way to press reset. It can focus attention on the pace and rhythm of young children's everyday experiences in ECEC and in so doing protect time for play and listening. As Cuffaro comments:

> children [are] given ample time and space for exploration and materials as means, the larger world is made accessible and manageable – slowed down sufficiently so that it might be held and probed in a variety of ways and personally understood.
>
> *(1995: 71)*

Thinking about slow can expand to a reconsidering of the relationship with time in early childhood and more widely in education, across sectors, including in higher education, seeking a timefull approach, not afraid to take the longer view. This debate is *not* about turning the clock back. It centres on prescient contemporary concerns that requires a reconceptualising of what ECEC can be:

> Our conception of pedagogy is dynamic, not mummified. Either pedagogy – like all the human sciences – is remade, reconstructed and updated based on the new conditions of the times, or it loses its nature, its function, its proper capacity to correspond to the times it lives in, and above all to foresee, anticipate and prepare the days of tomorrow.
>
> *(Malaguzzi, in Cagliari et al. 2016: 143)*

Paradoxically when we prioritise a slower pace it is easier to see what is urgent.

Questions

1 What would be your key points in developing different relationships with time in ECEC in the future?
2 If you were designing professional development on this topic where would you start?
3 What organisations or people do you think would be allies for the ECEC sector in valuing slow knowledge and the unhurried child?

Note

1 Kete is the Māori word for basket.

APPENDIX

This book has grown from the study: 'Slow Knowledge and the unhurried child' (2020–2021) funded by the Froebel Trust. It is based on in-depth interviews with the following participants (see Chapter 1).

Amanda Bateman, PhD, is an Associate Professor in Early Childhood Education and Director of the Early Years Research Centre at University of Waikato, New Zealand. Her research involves collecting and analysing video footage of children's social interactions, and teacher-child pedagogical interactions. She uses conversation analysis in her early childhood research to unpack in detail the interactions of the participants. Her recent publications include the co-edited books with Dr Amelia Church – *Early Childhood Education: The Co-Production of Knowledge and Relationships* and *Talking With Children: A Handbook for Early Childhood Education.*

Kari Carlsen, PhD, is Professor of Forming, Design and Art and Craft at the University of South-Eastern Norway (USN). She works with preschool teacher education and students at bachelor, master's and doctoral level. She founded the Norwegian Reggio Emilia Network in 1996 and is the Norwegian contact for the Reggio Children International network. She has been involved in continuing and further education of kindergarten teachers. Her three main research themes are: 1) Reggio Emilia-inspired work and pedagogical documentation, 2) exploring material and aesthetic learning processes and 3) curriculum research and framework factors for play and learning. She leads the research group Embodied Making and Learning – Early Childhood Education and Care (EMAL-ECE) at USN.

William Clark is a Key Stage One Phase leader with well-being and PHSCE responsibilities in an East London Primary school. Will has experience of teaching both early years and Key Stage One. He completed a Master's of Education dissertation about how storytelling and story acting might be used to bridge the divide between Reception and Year 1. Will has delivered training on working with 'Helicopter Stories' (Makebelieve Arts).

Kate Cowan, PhD, is a Lecturer in Education at the University of Sheffield and an Honorary Senior Research Fellow at IOE, UCL's Faculty for Education and Society. With a background in early years teaching, her research focuses on young children's play and communication from a multimodal perspective. Recent projects include 'A National Observatory of Children's Play Experiences During Covid-19' (funded by the ESRC), 'Playing the Archive: Memory, Community and Mixed Reality Play' (funded by the EPSRC), and 'Valuing Young Children's Signs of Learning: Observation and Digital Documentation of Play in Early Years Class-rooms' (funded by The Froebel Trust).

Emma Dyer, PhD, researches the value, management and design of small spaces in schools and how they can further benefit the children, young people and adults who use them. Emma edits and writes for architectureandeducation.org with Dr Adam Wood; a site that they established together in 2015. She also writes about spaces in schools where reading and where therapies take place in her own site pre-ciousspaces.org. *Precious Spaces* is based on previous research from her PhD (2018) about how to establish well-designed, supportive reading spaces for beginner read-ers in school. Her current collaborative research is with Dr Sara Freitag, Senior Educational Psychologist for Achieving for Children, about the design of thera-peutic spaces in schools. Emma also works with Achieving for Children Virtual School, advising and supporting schools and families of previously looked-after children and young people.

Biljana Fredriksen, PhD, is Professor of Art and Craft at University of South-Eastern Norway, Faculty of Humanities, Sports and Educational Science. She has been teaching at teacher education programs for 25 years, mainly at early childhood teacher education. Fredriksen's 2011 PhD-thesis *Negotiating grasp: embodied experi-ence with three-dimensional materials and the negotiation of meaning in early childhood education* investigates the significance of embodied, experiential forms of learn-ing through interactions and intra-actions among preschool children and materi-als. Her research interests further develop toward Murrishuman intra-actions with natural materials, experiential learning in more-than-humans and eco-pedagogical perspectives in teaching. Fredriksen has published two books in Norwegian, and number of articles and book chapters in English and Norwegian.

Deborah Harcourt, PhD, was the Foundation Professor of Early Childhood at the Australian Catholic University, in Queensland Australia and is now the Execu-tive Director for Asia Pacific Early Childhood Consultants. She has worked in the field of early childhood education for the past 30 years in Australia, Singapore (where she was based for ten years), China, Malaysia, India, Indonesia, UAE, UK and Sri Lanka. Deborah began her career as a preschool teacher, working with three-to-five-year-old children and then moved to the tertiary sector where she has taught at both undergraduate and postgraduate levels in teacher education, health sciences and within a school of medicine. She is interested in researching with young children to explore their views and opinions about matters that might concern them in order to uphold the UNCRC in research practice. Deborah is a long-term investigator of the principles of the Reggio Emilia Educational Project, and what they might mean to early childhood education outside of Italy.

Kari-Anne Jørgensen-Vittersø, PhD, is Associate Professor at Oslo Metropolitan University. Her research interests include childhood outdoor play and learning, sense of place, slow pedagogy and learning for sustainability. She gained a Doctorate in Philosophy at the University of Gothenburg. The title of her Doctoral thesis was: 'What is going on out there? What does it mean for children's experiences when the kindergarten is moving their everyday activities into the nature – landscape and its places?' Kari-Anne's recent research studies have focused on children, nature and culture in urban landscapes.

Karin Andrews Jashapara leads Forest School sessions in London, developing her practice in progressive education and the uses of art and play in the child/non-human relationship. For decades she designed and performed shadow puppet theatre for commissions about difficult subjects such as the human relationship with nature, death and catastrophic brain injury. Now she is more often found storytelling, with shadows and other visual languages at times, inspired by her reading, her colleagues and the woodlands.

Sylvia Kind, PhD, is a faculty instructor in Early Childhood Education at Capilano University and an *atelierista* at the Capilano University Children's Centre. Her work is grounded in a/r/tography, research-creation, and art practice as research, and is motivated by an interest in young children's studio practices, their lively material improvisations and collective experimentations, and in developing understandings of studio research in early childhood contexts and the implications for teacher education. She has co-authored the book *Encounters with Materials in Early Childhood Education,* co-edited *Drawing as Language,* and has written several journal articles and book chapters on studio practices in early childhood.

Mara Krechevsky is a senior researcher at Project Zero. Mara has been conducting educational research for over 35 years, including directing Making Learning Visible (MLV), an investigation into documenting and assessing individual and group learning from preschool to high school. MLV is based on collaborative research with educators from the municipal preschools in Reggio Emilia, Italy. Mara also co-directs the Cultivating Civic and Creative Capacities project, a collaboration with the Columbus Museum of Art and K-12 teachers in Ohio, and is a researcher on the Pedagogy of Play project, a collaboration with the Lego

Foundation to develop a pedagogy for supporting learning through play from preschool to middle school. Mara works with teachers and administrators in the United States and abroad on creating powerful learning environments for children and adults. Mara has authored or co-authored numerous articles and books, including *Visible Learners: Promoting Reggio-Inspired Approaches in All Schools* (Jossey-Bass, 2013) and *Making Learning Visible: Children as Individual and Group Learners* (Reggio Children, 2001).

Lynn McNair, PhD, is a Lecturer in Early Childhood Practice and Froebel/Research Fellow at the University of Edinburgh. Lynn has more than 40 years of experience working in early years education and was awarded an OBE for services to Early Education in 2009. Lynn is a trained Froebelian, attaining her certificate at the Froebel Institute, Roehampton University, London, UK. She is an award-winning author and was recently awarded a Principal Fellowship from the Higher Education Academy. Lynn would say her passion for egalitarianism, emancipation, democracy and a belief that children are rich, active, resourceful beings came from being a mother to Kurt and Mischa; and what she learned as she observed them playing freely as children. This way of being with children, trusting in them in their abilities and capabilities is where she puts her energy into her work with children today.

Mari Mori, EdD, is Professor of Early Childhood Education at Kobe Shinwa Women's University, Japan. She gained her Doctor of Education at Teachers College, Columbia University, USA. Mari has taught in kindergartens in Tokyo, Japan, and New York City, USA. She is a Board Director of the Japanese National Committee of OMEP and has served as Coordinator of Reggio International Network. Her research interests focus on children's artistic thinking, children's rights and practice, and pedagogical documentation.

Peter Moss is an Emeritus Professor of Early Childhood Provision at the Institute of Education, University College London. For many years he was the co-editor of the Contesting Early Childhood series. His most recent book in the series is *Neoliberalism and Early Childhood Education: Markets, Imaginaries and Governance*, co-authored with Guy Roberts-Holmes.

Solveig Nordtømme, PhD, is an Associate Professor in kindergarten pedagogy at the University of South-Eastern Norway. Her research interest is related to how places, space and materiality are included in pedagogical practices and play. She has written several articles and book chapters on the theme of play, space, and materiality in kindergarten. She teaches in Early Childhood Education (ECE) on bachelor and master's degrees, and her topics are children as actors, pedagogical documentation, learning theories and kindergarten space and materiality.

Júlia Oliveira-Formosinho is Professor of Early Childhood Education at the University of Minho and the Catholic University of Portugal. She is joint Director of research at the Childhood Association (Associaçâo Criança), a civic network, promoting a sociocultural-constructivist approach to the education of children and teachers and advocacy of children's rights. Júlia is a member of the Board of Trustees of the EECERA (European Early Childhood Education Research Association) and coordinator of the Special Issues of EECERA Journal. Since 1996 onwards she has been the editor of a series for the leading educational publishing house in Portugal and in African Portuguese-speaking countries: Porto Editora, called 'Childhood Series'. Júlia's own publications include several books, book chapters and research articles.

Mari Pettersvold, PhD, is Associate Professor in sociology at the University of South-Eastern Norway. She has published articles and books about democracy in ECEC, both with regard to the children and the professional practitioners. Her research interests focus on the conditions that make democracy possible, and those that make democracy difficult. Mari teaches on a master's programme in Pedagogy with a focus on kindergarten management.

Tahmina Shayan is an instructor in the School of Childhood Studies at Capilano University. She has a Master of Science in art education and Master of Education in curriculum and instruction from Pennsylvania State University. Her work studies the ways in which local and global discourses shape and impact early childhood curriculum and teachers' pedagogical practices and the implication of such practices on children's learning and being. Her areas of research include children's artistic practices, studio spaces, cultural studies, globalisation, teacher education, curriculum and pedagogy.

Persille Schwartz works as chief adviser and team leader at the Danish Ministry of Children and Education offering national guidance to local authorities on how to supervise quality development in daycare and ECEC-centres. She has wide experience of a range of positions and tasks related to ECEC-development, including pedagogical practice, teaching students and pedagogues/staff and participation in research and development projects. Persille has contributed to development of local, national and EU-quality frameworks for ECEC. She has a keen interest and a strong voice in supporting children voices in being valued as an unavoidable and essential element as adults strive for improving the physical, mental and aesthetical learning environments of ECEC-settings. Persille initiated a development study with Alison Clark and colleagues from the Danish Evaluation Institute to explore adapting the Mosaic approach to a Danish cultural context.

Clodie Tal, PhD, is a developmental psychologist involved in Teacher Education in ECEC. The preparation and in-service "training" of caregivers and teachers working with young children are perceived by her as an ongoing preventive intervention; as means of improving the conditions of life of young children coming from diverse backgrounds and for improving the odds for those coming from unprivileged backgrounds to build meaningful lives. She was the Head of the Master's degree in Early Childhood Education and before that she headed the Bachelor's degree in Education at Levinsky College of Education Tel Aviv, Israel. Currently she is a lecturer-professor at the Achva and Hemdat-Darom Colleges in Israel. Her main areas of interest which are also the focus of her research include: teacher–child and teacher–parent relationships, teachers' values, promoting children's social competence and coping with behaviour problems, classroom management and teacher–children dialogic discourse in general, with a focus on children picture-books in particular.

REFERENCES

Adam, B., 2000. The temporal gaze: The challenge for social theory in the context of GM food. *The British Journal of Sociology*, 51 (1), 125–142.

Albin-Clark, J., 2020. What is documentation doing? Early childhood education teachers shifting from and between the meanings and actions of documentation practices. *Contemporary Issues in Early Childhood Education*, 22 (2), 140–155. https://doi.org/10.1177/1463949120917157.

Aoki, T., 1983/2005. Curriculum implementation as instrumental action and as situational praxis. *In:* W. Pinar and R. Irwin, eds. *Curriculum in a new key: The collected works of Ted T. Aoki*. Mahwah, NJ: Lawrence Erlbaum, 111–123. https://doi.org/10.4324/9781410611390.

Archer, N., 2021. 'I have this subversive curriculum underneath': Narratives of micro resistance in early childhood education study on resistance. *Journal of Early Childhood Education*, 20 (3), 431–445. https://doi.org/10.1177/1476718x211059907.

Atkinson, D., 2011. *Art, equality and learning: Pedagogies against the state*. Rotterdam: Sense.

Atkinson, D., 2015. The adventure of pedagogy, learning and the not-known. *Subjectivity*, 8, 43–56. https://doi.org/10.1057/sub.2014.22.

Bachelard, G., 1994. *The poetics of space*. Translated by Maria Jolas. Boston, MA: Beacon Press.

Badyer-Saye, S., 2006. Figuring time: Providence and politics. *In:* R. Rashkover and C. C. Pecknold, eds. *Liturgy, time and the politics of redemption*. London: SCM Press, 91–111.

Bakhtin, M., 1981. Discourse in the novel (M. Holquist and C. Emerson, Trans.). *In:* M. Holquist, ed. *The dialogic imagination*. Austin: University of Texas Press, 259–422.

Ball, S., 2010. New voices, new knowledges and new politics of educational research: The gathering of a perfect storm? *European Educational Research Journal*, 9 (2), 124–137.

Ball, S., 2016. Neoliberal education? Confronting the slouching beast. *Policy Futures in Education*, 14 (8), 1046–1059.

Bateman, A., 2015. *Conversation analysis and early childhood: The co-production of knowledge and relationships*. London and New York: Routledge.

Bath, C., 2012. 'I can't read it; I don't know': Young children's participation in the pedagogical documentation of English early childhood education and care settings. *International*

Journal of Early Years Education, 20 (2), 190–201. https://doi.org/10.1080/09669760.20
12.715242.

Beery, T., and Jørgensen, K. A., 2018. Children in nature: Sensory engagement and the experience of biodiversity. *Environmental Education Research*, 24 (1), 13–25. https://doi.org/10.1080/13504622.2016.1250149.

Biesta, G., 2012. The educational significance of the experience of resistance: Schooling and the dialogue between child and world. *Other Education: The Journal of Educational Alternatives*, 1 (1), 92–103.

Biesta, G., 2013. *The beautiful risk of education*. Boulder, CO: Paradigm Publishing.

Bjornerud, M., 2018. *Timefulness: How thinking like a geologist can help save the world*. Princeton, NJ: Princeton University Press.

Bjornerud, M., and Claus, A. K., 2018. *Interview with Marcia Bjornerud: Timefulness: A Geologist's story – Interview with Marcia Bjornerud*. Available from: https://humansandnature.org/timefulness-interview-with-marcia-bjornerud/.

Blaisdell, C., McNair, L. J., Addison, L., and Davis, J. M., 2021. 'Why am I in all of these pictures?' From Learning Stories to Lived Stories: The politics of children's participation rights in documentation practices. *European Early Childhood Education Research Journal*, 30, 572–585. https://doi.org/10.1080/1350293x.2021.2007970.

Bosanquet, A., Mantai, L., and Fredericks, V., 2020. Deferred time in the neoliberal university: Experiences of doctoral candidates and early career academics. *Teaching in Higher Education*, 25 (6), 736–749. https://doi.org/10.1080/13562517.2020.1759528.

Bourdieu, P., 1997. The forms of capital. *In:* A. Halsey, H. Lauder, P. Brown and A. Wells, eds. *Education, culture. Economy and society*. Oxford: Oxford University Press, 241–258.

Bradbury, A., 2019. Datafied at four: The role of data in the 'schoolification' of early childhood education in England. *Learning, Media and Technology*, 44 (1), 7–21.

Brogaard Clausen, S., Guimaraes, S., Howe, S., and Cottle, M., 2015. Assessment of young children on entry to school: Informative, formative or performative? *Journal for Cross-Disciplinary Subjects in Education*, 6 (1), 2120–2125.

Bronfenbrenner, U., 1979. *The ecology of human development*. Cambridge, MA: Harvard University Press.

Brooker, L., 2002. *Starting school: Young children learning cultures*. Buckingham: Open University Press.

Brosterman, N., 1997. *Inventing kindergarten*. London: Harry N. Abrams.

Bruce, T., 1991. *Time to play in early childhood education*. London: Hodder & Stoughton.

Bruce, T., 2016. Friedrich Froebel. *In:* T. David, K. Goouch and S. Powell, eds. *The Routledge handbook of philosophies and theories of early childhood education and care*. London: Routledge, 19–25.

Bruce, T., 2017. Ponderings on play: Froebelian assemblages. *In:* T. Bruce, P. Hakkarinen and M. Bredikyte, eds. *The Routledge handbook of early childhood play*. London: Routledge, 9–21.

Bruce, T., 2020. *Educating young children: A lifetime journey into a Froebelian approach. The selected works of Tina Bruce*. London: Routledge.

Bruce, T., McNair, L., and Whinnett, J., eds. 2020. *Putting storytelling at the heart of early childhood practice: A reflective guide for early years practitioners*. London: Routledge.

Bruner, J. S., 1960. *The process of education*. Cambridge, MA: Harvard University Press.

Burke, C., 2013. *A life in education and architecture: Mary Beaumont Medd*. Farnham: Ashgate Publishing.

Burke, C., and Grosvenor, I., 2003. *The school I'd like: Children's and young people's reflections on education for the 21st century*. London: RoutledgeFalmer.

Cagliari, P., Castagnetti, M., Giudici, C., Rinaldi, C., Vecchi, V., and Moss, P., eds. 2016. *Loris Malaguzzi and schools of Reggio Emilia: A selection of his writings and speeches, 1945–1993.* London: Routledge.

Calvino, I., 1997. *Invisible cities.* London: Vintage Classics.

Cameron, C., 2020 Towards recognising practitioners working in out-of-home care as experts in everyday life: A conceptual critique. *International Journal of Social Pedagogy,* 9 (1), 19. https://doi.org/10.14324/111.444.ijsp.2020.v9.x.019.

Cameron, C., and Moss, P., 2007. *Care work in Europe: Current understandings and future directions.* London: Routledge.

Cameron, C., and Moss, P., eds. 2011. *Social pedagogy and working with children and young people.* London: Jessica Kingsley Press.

Cameron, C., and Moss, P., eds. 2020. *Transforming early childhood in England: Towards a democratic education.* London: UCL Press, 134–150.

Cameron, C., Moss, P., and Petrie, P., 2021. Towards a social pedagogic approach for social care. *International Journal of Social Pedagogy,* 10 (1), 7. https://doi.org/10.14324/111.444.ijsp.2021.v10.x.007.

Campbell, J., and Neill, S., 1994. *Curriculum reform at key stage 1: Teacher commitment and policy failure.* Harlow: Longman, in association with the Association of Teachers and Lecturers.

Canning, N., 2019. 'Just five more minutes': Power dynamics in outdoor play. *International Journal of Play,* 8 (1), 11–24. https://doi.org/10.1080/21594937.2019.1580332.

Carlsen, K., 2015. *Forming I barnehager I lys av Reggio Emilias atelierkultur.* Åbo: Åbo Akademi University Press.

Carlsen, K., 2021. *Reggio Emilia: atelierkultur og utforskende pedagogikk.* Bergen: Fagbokforlaget.

Carlsen, K., and Clark, A., 2022. Potentialities of pedagogical documentation as an intertwined research process with children and teachers in slow pedagogies. *European Early Childhood Education Research Journal,* 30 (2), 200–212. https://doi.org/10.1080/1350293X.2022.2046838.

Carr, M., Jones, C., and Lee, W., 2005. Beyond listening: Can assessment practice play a part? *In:* A. Clark, A. Kjørholt and P. Moss, eds. *Beyond listening: Children's perspectives on early childhood services.* Bristol: Policy Press, 129–150.

Carr, M., and Lee, W., 2019. Learning stories: Pedagogical practices and provocations. *In:* J. Formosinho and J. Peeters, eds. *Understanding pedagogic documentation in early childhood education: Revealing and reflecting on high quality learning and teaching.* London: Routledge, 4–31.

Clark, A., 2010a. *Transforming children's spaces: Children's and adults' participation in designing learning environments.* London: Routledge.

Clark, A., 2010b. 'In-between' spaces in postwar primary schools: A micro-study of a 'welfare room' (1977–1993). *History of Education,* 39 (6), 767–778.

Clark, A., 2011. Multi-modal map making with young children: Exploring ethnographic and participatory methods. *Qualitative Research,* 11 (3), 311–330.

Clark, A., 2012. *Ways of knowing: Developing the Mosaic approach with young children and adults* (PhD by Published Work). Milton Keynes: The Open University.

Clark, A., 2014. 'Developing and adapting the Mosaic approach'. *In:* A. Clark, R. Flewitt, M. Hammersley and M. Robb, eds. *Understanding Research with Children and Young People.* London: Sage, 200–209.

Clark, A., 2017. *Listening to young children: A guide to understanding and using the mosaic approach.* London: Jessica Kingsley.

Clark, A., 2019a. Å forbli nysgjerrig på barn med foto. Barns fotografiske ytringer, Barnehagefolk, (3), 68–75.

Clark, A., 2019b. Quilting' with the Mosaic approach: Smooth and striated spaces in early childhood research. *Journal of Early Childhood Education Research,* 8 (2), 236–251.

Clark, A., 2020. Towards a listening ECEC system. *In:* C. Cameron and P. Moss, eds. *Transforming early childhood in England: Towards a democratic education.* London: UCL Press, 134–150.

Clark, A., and Flewitt, R., 2020. The competent child: Valuing all young children as knowledgeable commentators on their own lives. *Review of Science, Mathematics and ICT Education,* 14 (2), 9–24.

Clark, A., Kjørholt, A., and Moss, P., 2005. *Beyond listening: Children's perspectives on early childhood services.* Bristol: Policy Press.

Clark, A., and Moss, P., 2001. *Listening to young children: The Mosaic approach.* London: National Children's Bureau for the Joseph Rowntree Foundation.

Clark, A., and Moss, P., 2005. *Spaces to play: More listening to young children using the Mosaic approach.* London: National Children's Bureau.

Clay, M., 1993. *Reading recovery: A guidebook for teachers in training.* London: Heinemann Educational.

Clay, M., 2019. *An observation survey of early literacy achievement.* 4th ed. New York: Scholastic.

Collett, K. S., van den Berg, C. L., Verster, B., and Bozalek, V., 2018. Incubating a slow pedagogy in professional academic development: An ethics of care perspective. *South African Journal of Higher Education,* 32 (6), 117–136.

Common Worlds Research Collective, 2019. Commonworlds, childhoods and pedagogies. Available from: http://commonworlds.net/about-the collective/ [Accessed 14 February 2022].

Compton-Lilly, C., 2015. Time in education: Intertwined dimensions and theoretical possibilities. *Time and Society,* 25 (3), 575–593. https://doi.org/10.1177/0961463X15587837.

Cook, T., and Hess, E., 2007. What the camera sees and from whose perspective: Fun methodologies for engaging children in enlightening adults. *Childhood,* 14 (1), 29–45.

Cousins, J., 1999. *Listening to four year olds: How they can help us plan their education and care.* London: National Early years Network.

Cowan, K., and Flewitt, R., 2021. Moving from paper-based to digital documentation in Early Childhood Education: Democratic potentials and challenges. *International Journal of Early Years Education,* 1–19. https://doi.org/10.1080/09669760.2021.2013171.

Cowan, K., Potter, J., Olusoga, Y., Bannister, C., Bishop, J. C., Cannon, M., and Signorelli, V., 2021. Children's digital play during the Covid 19 pandemic: Insights from the play observatory. *Journal of e-Learning and Knowledge Society,* 17 (3), 8–17.

Cowie, B., and Carr, M., 2004. The consequences of sociocultural assessment. *In:* A. Anning, J. Cullen and M. Fleer, eds. *Early Childhood Education: Society and Culture.* London: SAGE.

Cross, B., 2011. Becoming, being and having been: Perspectives on temporal stances and participation across children's services. *Children & Society,* 25 (1), 26–36.

Csikszentmihalyi, M., 1990. *Flow: The psychology of optimal experience.* New York: Harper and Row.

Csikszentmihalyi, M., 1997. *Finding flow: The psychology of engagement with everyday life.* New York: Basic Books.

Cuffaro, H., 1995. *Experimenting with the world: John Dewey and the early childhood classroom.* New York: Teachers College Press.

Dahlberg, G., Moss, P., and Pence, A., 2013. *Beyond quality in early childhood education and care: Languages of evaluation.* 3rd ed. London: Routledge.

de Certeau, M., 1998. *The practice of everyday life.* Berkeley, CA: University of California Press.

Deleuze, G., and Guattari, F., 2004. *A thousand plateaus: Capitalism and schizophrenia.* Translated by Brian Massumi, 2nd ed. London: Continuum.

Department for Education, 2021. *Statutory framework for the early years foundation stage: Setting the standards for learning, development and care for children from birth to five.* London: Department for Education.

Department for Education and Employment, 1998. *The national literacy strategy: Framework for teaching.* London: Department for Education and Employment.

Driscoll, V., and Rudge, C., 2005. Channels for listening to young children and parents. In: A. Clark, A. Kjørholt and P. Moss, eds. *Beyond listening: Children's perspectives on early childhood services.* Bristol: Policy Press, 91–110.

Drummond, M. J., 2000. Comparisons in early years education: History, fact and fiction. *Early Childhood Research and Practice,* 2 (1, Spring). Available from: http://ecrp.uiuc.edu/v2n1/print/drummond.html [Accessed 14 February 2022].

Dyer, E., 2018a. Designing the 'in-between': Alison Clark's micro-history of a welfare room. *Architecture and Education,* 8 May. Available from: https://architectureandeducation.org/2018/05/08/designing-the-in-between-alison-clarks-micro-history-of-a-welfare-room/ [Accessed 9 February 2022].

Dyer, E., 2018b. Where do beginner readers read in the English, mainstream primary school and where could they read? (Doctoral thesis). https://doi.org/10.17863/CAM.25558.

Edwards, C., Gandini, L., and Forman, G., eds. 2012. *The Hundred languages of Children.* 3rd ed. Santa Barbara, CA: Praeger.

Eistrup, A., ed., 2016. *Håndbog i børneinddragelse.* København: Børnerådet.

Elfer, P., and Selleck, D., 1999. *The best of both worlds: Enhancing the experiences of young children in the nursery.* Unpublished paper. London: National Children's Bureau.

Elkind, D., 1981. *The hurried child: Growing up too fast, too soon.* 25th anniversary ed. Cambridge, MA: Da Capos Press.

Fawcett, M., and Watson, D., 2016. *Learning through child observation.* 3rd ed. London: Jessica Kingsley Publishers.

Ferguson, D., 2020. Don't turn your home into school . . . the Lego professor of play on lockdown learning. *The Guardian,* 21 April. Available from: www.theguardian.com/education/2020/apr/21/dont-turn-your-home-into-school-lego-prof-of-play-on-lockdown-learning [Accessed 20 January 2022].

Fisher, R., 2020. Welcome to the Long-termist's field guide. Available from: https://longtermist.substack.com/p/welcome-to-the-long-termists-field.

Fisher, R., 2023. *The long view: How to escape the age of Short-termism.* London: Wildfire Press.

Fleet, A., Patterson, C., Robertson, J., and Robertson, J., eds. 2017. *Pedagogical documentation in early years practice: Seeing through multiple perspectives.* London: SAGE.

Flewitt, R., and Cowan, K., 2019. *Valuing young children's signs of learning: Observation and digital documentation of play in early years classrooms.* Final Report. Roehampton: The Froebel Trust.

Flewitt, R., Cremin, T., and Mardell, B., 2017. Paley's approach to storytelling and story acting: Research and practice. In: T. Cremin, R. Flewitt, B. Mardell and J. Swann, eds. *Storytelling in early childhood: Enriching language, literacy and classroom culture.* London: Routledge, 29–48.

Formosinho, J., and Oliveira-Formosinho, J., 2008. *Pedagogy-in-participation: Childhood association's approach.* Research report. Lisbon: Aga Khan Foundation.

Formosinho, J., and Oliveira-Formosinho, J., 2016. The search for a holistic approach to evaluation. In: J. Oliveira-Formosinho and C. Pascal, eds. *Assessment and evaluation for transformation in early childhood.* London: Routledge, 93–106.

Formosinho, J., and Peeters, J. eds. 2019. *Understanding pedagogic documentation in early childhood education: Revealing and reflecting on high quality learning and teaching.* London: Routledge.

Foucault, M., 1993. About the Beginning of the Hermeneutics of the Self. (Transcription of two lectures in Darthmouth on Nov. 17 and 24, 1980., ed. by Mark Blasius). *Political Theory,* 21 (2), 198–227.

Froebel, F., 1867. *The education of man.* Translated by R. Hailmann. New York: Appleton.

Gadamer, H. G., 1975. *Truth and method.* London: Blackwell.

Galimberti, U., 2008. 'Generazioni a confronto', Republica delle Donne, 5 March 2008.

Gallacher, L., In Press. From milestones to wayfaring: Geographic metaphors and iconography of embodied growth and change in infancy and early childhood. *GeoHumanities*.

Gee, J., 1999. New people in new worlds: Networks, the new capitalism and schools. *In:* B. Cope and M. Kalantzis, eds. *Multiliteracies: Literacy learning and the design of social futures*. London: Routledge.

Giamminuti, S., 2013. *Dancing with Reggio Emilia: Metaphors for quality*. Mt Victoria, NSW: Pademelon Press.

Gillen, J., and Cameron, C. A., eds. 2010. *International perspectives on early childhood research: A day in the life*. Basingstoke: Palgrave Macmillan.

Giudici, C., and Krechevsky, M., eds. 2001. *Making learning visible: Children as individual and group learners*. Reggio Emilia: Reggio Children.

Grant, H., 2021. Paediatricians call for Covid rules to ease so children can play. *The Guardian*. February 14. Available from: www.theguardian.com/society/2021/feb/14/paediatricians-call-for-covid-rules-to-ease-so-children-can-play [Accessed 21 January 2022].

Grimmett, P., 2022. Interlude: The inspirited curriculum. *In:* N. Lee, L. Wong and J. Ursino, eds. *Lingering with the works of Ted Aoki: Historical and contemporary significance for curriculum research and practice*. New York: Routledge, 156–158.

Guard, C., 2021. *The undiscovered stories of the babyroom: Exploring infant and practitioner voices during social encounters in the nursery*. *In:* Froebel 2021: Visions of social justice, equity and integrity in the year of childhood. 9th Biennial International Froebel Society Conference, 1–4th June. University of Edinburgh.

Hackett, A., 2015. Young children as wayfarers: Learning about place by moving through it. *Children & Society*, 30 (3), 169–179. https://doi.org/10.1111/chso.12130.

Hackett, A., Holmes, R., and, MacRae, C., eds. 2020. *Working with young children in museums: Weaving theory and practice*. London: Routledge.

Han, B. C., 2017. *The scent of time: A philosophical essay on the art of lingering*. Translated by D. Steuer. New York: Polity Press.

Hansen, H. K., and Jensen J. J., 2004. *A study of understandings in care and pedagogical practice: Experiences using the Sophos model in cross national studies consolidated report*. Work Package 10. Carework in Europe. London: Thomas Coram Research Unit.

Hansen, S. R., Hansen, M. W., and Kristensen, N. H., 2017. Striated agency and smooth regulation: Kindergarten mealtime as an ambiguous space for the construction of child and adult relations. *Children's Geographies*, 15 (2), 237–248.

Harrison-Greaves, J., 2016. Slow education leads to rich and balanced learning. Available from: www.bera.ac.uk/blog/slow-education-leads-to-rich-and-balanced-learning [Accessed 14 February 2022].

Hart, R., 1997. *Children's participation: The theory and practice of involving young citizens in community development and environmental care*. New York: Routledge.

Hay, P., 2018. *School without walls 2010–2018*. Bath: 5x5x5 =creativity. http://researchspace.bathspa.ac.uk/id/eprint/12275 [Accessed 30 March 2022].

Hohmann, M., Banet, B., and Weikart, D. P., 1979. *Young children in action: A manual for preschool educators: The cognitively oriented preschool curriculum*. Ypsilanti, MI: High/Scope Press.

Hole, S., 2009. *Dem gamle mannen og hvalen* [The Old Man and the Whale]. Oslo: Cappelen Damm.

Holt, M., 2002. It's time to start the slow school movement. Phi Delta Kappan, 84, 265–271.

Honoré, C., 2004. *In praise of slow: How a worldwide movement is challenging the cult of speed*. London: Orion Books.

Horsley, K., 2021. Slowing down: Documentary photography in early childhood. *International Journal of Early Years Education*, 29 (4), 438–454. https://doi.org/ 10.1080/09669760. 2020.1850430.

Horsley, K., 2022. Exploring young migrant children's 'funds of knowledge' through documentary photography (EdD thesis awarded March). Milton Keynes: The Open University.

Ingold, T., 2012. *Thinking through making. Presentation from the Institute for Northern Culture 'Tales from the North.'* Lapland University Consortium (LUC), Finland. Viewed at: https://www.youtube.com/watch?v=Ygne72-4zyo. Accessed October 2022.

Ingold, T., 2015. *The life of lines*. London: Routledge.

Irwin, R., 2013. Becoming a/r/tography. *Studies in Art Education*, 54 (3), 198–215.

Jardine, D., 2008. On the while of things. *Journal of American Association for Advancement of Curriculum Studies*, 4, unpaginated. Available from: https://ojs.library.ubc.ca/index.php/jaaacs/article/view/187726/185831.

Jardine, D., 2013. Time is (not) always running out. *Journal of the American Association for the Advancement of Curriculum Studies*, 9 (2), unpaginated. Available from: https://ojs.library.ubc.ca/index.php/jaaacs/article/view/187726/185831.

Jardine, D., 2012. *Introduction: "Left in peace". Pedagogy left in peace: Cultivating free spaces in teaching and learning*. London: Continuum, 1–22. Bloomsbury Collections. Web. 6 May 2021. http://dx.doi.org/10.5040/9781472541239.0003.

Jarvis, P., 2020. The myth of early acceleration. *In:* S. Palmer ed. *Play is the way: child development, early years and the future of Scottish education*. Paisley: CCWB Press, 42–50.

Jensen, J. J., 2011. Understandings of Danish pedagogical practice. *In:* C. Cameron and P. Moss, eds. *Social pedagogy and working with children and young people*. London: Jessica Kingsley Press, 141–147.

Jensen, J. J., 2017. Denmark – ECEC Workforce Profile. In: P. Oberhuemer and I. Schreyer, eds. Workforce profiles in systems of early childhood education and care in Europe. www.seepro.eu/English/Country_Reports.htm.

Jewitt, C., and Jones, K., 2005. Managing time and space in the new English classroom. *In:* M. Lawn and I. Grosvenor, eds. *Materialities of schooling: Design, technology, objects, routines*. Oxford: Symposium Books, 201–214.

Jørgensen, K. A., 2016. Bringing the jellyfish home: Environmental consciousness and 'sense of wonder' in young children's encounters with natural landscapes and places'. *Environmental Education Research*, 22 (8), 1139–1157.

Kalkman, K., and Clark, A., 2017. Here we like playing princesses – newcomer migrant children's transitions within day care: Exploring role play as an indication of suitability and home and belonging. *European Early Childhood Education Research Journal*, 25 (2), 292–304. https://doi.org/10.1080/1350293X.2017.1288020.

Kind, S., Shayan, T., and Cameron, C., 2019. Lingering in artistic spaces: Becoming attuned to children's processes and perspectives through the early childhood studio. *In:* C. Patterson and L. Kocher, eds. *Pedagogies for children's perspectives*. London: Routledge, 67–80.

Krechevsky, M. with Baldwin, M., Rodriguez, M. C., Christensen, L., Jorgensen, M., Jorgensen, O., Krishnadas, S., Overgaard, S., and Rabenhoj, T., 2019. "Frankly It's a Gamble": What happens when middle school students compose their own schedules? *Scottish Educational Review*, 51 (2), 71–89.

Laevers, F., 2000. Forward to basics! Deep-level-learning and the experiential approach. *Early Years*, 20 (2), 20–29. https://doi.org/10.1080/0957514000200203.

Laevers, F., 2015. *Making care and education more effective through wellbeing and involvement. An introduction to experiential education*. Belgium: Research Centre for Experiential Education – University of Leuven. Available from: www.gov.gg/CHttpHandler.ashx?id=121630&p=0.

Lasczik Cutcher, A., and Irwin, R. L., 2017. Walkings-through paint: A c/a/r/tography of slow scholarship. *Journal of Curriculum and Pedagogy*, 14 (2), 116–124. https://doi.org/10.1080/15505170.2017.1310680.

Lee, N., Wong, L., and Ursino, J., 2022. Introduction: Aokian notes and intergenerational resonances. *In:* N. Lee, L. Wong and J. Ursino, eds. *Lingering with the works of Ted Aoki: Historical and contemporary significance for curriculum research and practice.* New York: Routledge, 1–16.

Lee, T., 2015. *Princesses, dragons and Helicopter Stories; storytelling and story acting in the early years.* London: Routledge.

Lee, T., 2022. *The growth of the storyteller: Helicopter stories in action.* London: Routledge.

Lefebvre, H., 1991. *Critique of everyday life.* Translated by John Moore. London: Verso.

Lefebvre, H., 2013. *Rhythmanalysis: Space, time and everyday life.* Translated by Stuart Elden and Gerald Moore. London: Bloomsbury Academic.

Lemke, J. L., 2000. Across the scales of time: Artefacts, activities and meanings in ecosocial systems. *Mind, Culture and Activity,* 7 (4), 273–290.

Lenz Taguchi, H., 2010. *Going beyond the theory/practice divide in early childhood education: Introducing an intra-active pedagogy.* London: Routledge.

Liebschner, J., 1992. *A child's work: Freedom and play in Froebel's educational theory and practice.* Cambridge: Lutterworth Press.

MacRae, C., 2019. Grace taking form. *Video Journal of Education and Pedagogy,* 4 (1), 151–166. Available from: https://doi.org/10.1163/23644583-00401003 [Accessed 14 February 2022].

MacRae, C., Hackett, A., and Holmes, A., 2021. Introduction to Part III. *In:* A. Hackett, R. Holmes and C. MacRae, eds. *Working with young children in museums: Weaving theory and practice.* London: Routledge, 135–143.

MacRae, C., Hackett, A., and Holmes, R., 2020. Introduction to Part III. *In:* A. Hackett, R. Holmes and C. MacRae, eds. *Working with young children in museums: Weaving theory and practice.* London: Routledge, 135–143.

Magrini, J. M., 2015. Phenomenology and curriculum implementation: Discerning a living curriculum through the analysis of Ted Aoki's situational praxis. *Journal of Curriculum Studies,* 47 (2), 274–299. https://doi.org/10.1080/00220272.2014.1002113.

Mardell, B., Wilson, D., Ryan, J., Ertel, K., Krechevsky, M., and Baker, M., 2016. *Towards a pedagogy of play: A project zero working paper.* Available from: http://pz.harvard.edu/sites/default/files/Towards%20a%20Pedagogy%20of%20Play.pdf [Accessed 11 February 2022].

Massey, D., 2002. Editorial: Time to think. *Transactions of the Institute of British Geographers,* 27 (3), 259–261.

May, W., 2000. The arts and curriculum as lingering. *In:* G. Willis and W. H. Schubert, eds. *Reflections from the heart of educational inquiry.* Troy: Educators International Press, 140–152.

McLaren, P., 2005. Critical pedagogy and class struggle in the age of neoliberal globalization: Notes from history's underside. *The International Journal of Inclusive Democracy,* 2 (1), 1–24.

McNair, L. J., Blaisdell, C., David, J. M., and Addison, J. L., 2021. Acts of pedagogical resistance: Marking out an ethical boundary against human technologies. *Policy Futures in Education,* 19 (4) 478–492.

McNair, l., and Powell, S., 2021. Friedrich Froebel: A path least trodden. *Early Child Development and Care,* 191 (7–8), 1175–1185. https://doi.org/10.1080/03004430.2020.1803299.

Merewether, J., 2018. Listening to young children outdoors with pedagogical documentation. *International Journal of Early Years Education,* 26 (3), 259–277.

Merewether, J., 2019. New materialisms and children's outdoor environments: Murmurative diffractions. *Children's Geographies,* 17 (1), 105–117. https://doi.org/10.1080/14733285.2018.1471449.

Merewether, J., 2020. Enchanted animism: A matter of care. *Contemporary Issues in Early Childhood*. https://doi.org/ 10.1177/1463949120971380.

Millei, Z., and Rautio, P., 2017. Overspills' of research with children: An argument for slow research. *Children's Geographies*, 15 (4), 466–477.

Mitchelmore, S., 2021. Lingering in an attitude of research: The critical potential of quotidien practices in early childhood education. *Contemporary Issues in Early Childhood*, 22 (1), 59–75.

Mitchelmore, S., Degotardi, S., and Fleet, A., 2017. The richness of everyday moments: Bringing visibility to the qualities of care within pedagogical spaces. *In:* E. White and C. Dalli, eds. *Under-three year olds in policy and practice. Policy and pedagogy with under-three year olds: Cross-disciplinary insights and innovations.* Singapore: Springer. https://doi.org/10.1007/978-981-10-2275-3_6.

Moss, P., 2010. Foreward. *In:* A. Clark, ed. *Transforming children's spaces: Children's and adults' participation in designing learning environments.* London: Routledge, xi–xiii.

Moss, P., 2019. *Alternative narratives in early childhood: An introduction for students and practitioners.* London: Routledge.

Mountz, A., Bonds, A., Mansfield, B., Loyd, J., Hyndman, J., Walton-Roberts, M., Basu, R., Whitson, R., Hawkins, R., Hamilton, T., and Curran, W., 2015. For slow scholarship: A feminist politics of resistance through collective action in the Neoliberal University. *ACME: An International Journal for Critical Geographies*, 14 (4), 1235–1259. Available from: www.acme-journal.org/index.php/acme/article/view/1058 [Accessed 7 February 2022].

Murris, K., and Kohan, T., 2021. Troubling troubled school time: Posthuman multiple temporalities. *International Journal of Qualitative Studies in Education*, 34 (7), 581–597. https://doi.org/10.1080/09518398.2020.1771461.

Norris Webb, R., 2014. The wisdom of re-vision. *In:* A. Webb and R. Norris Webb, eds. *On street photography and the poetic image.* New York: Aperture, 90.

O'Flynn, G., and Petersen, E. B., 2007. The 'good life' and the 'rich portfolio': Young women, schooling and neo-liberal subjectification. *British Journal of Sociology of Education*, 28 (4), 459–472.

Oliveira-Formosinho, J., and de Sousa, J., 2019. Developing pedagogic documentation: Children and educators learning the narrative mode. *In:* J. Formosinho and J. Peeters, eds. *Understanding pedagogic documentation in early childhood education.* London: Routledge, 32–51.

Olsson, L. M., 2009. *Movement and experimentation in young children's learning: Deleuze and Guattari in early childhood education.* London: Routledge.

O'Neill, M., 2014. The slow university – Work, time, and well-being. *Discover Society*, 3 June. Available from: www.discoversociety.org/2014/06/03/the-slow-university-work-time-and-well-being/ [Accessed 10 February 2022].

Orr, D. W., 1996. Slow knowledge. *Conservation Biology*, 10 (3), 699–702.

Osgood, J., 2009. Childcare workforce reform in England and 'the early years professional': A critical discourse analysis. *Journal of Education Policy*, 24 (6), 733–751.

Pacini-Ketchabaw, V., 2012. Acting with the clock: Clocking practices in early childhood. *Contemporary Issues in Early Childhood*, 13 (2), 154–160. https://doi.org/10.2304/ciec.2012.13.2.154.

Pacini-Ketchabaw, V., Kind, S., and Kocher, L., 2017. *Encounters with materials in early childhood education.* New York: Routledge.

Pacini-Ketchabaw, V., and Montpetit, M., 2019. More-than-human kinship relations with Indigenous children's picture books. *In:* F. Nxumalo and C. Brown, eds. *Disrupting and countering deficits in early childhood education.* New York: Routledge, 136–150.

Pacini-Ketchabaw, V., Nxumalo, F., Kocher, L., Elliot, E., and Sanchez, A., 2015. *Journeys: Reconceptualising early childhood practices through pedagogical narration*. Toronto: University of Toronto Press.

Pahl, K., 2020. Play is educational too: An alternative look at learning during lockdown. *Manchester Metropolitan University, Faculty of Education News*, 20 April. www.mmu.ac.uk/education/about-us/news/story/?id=12197 [Accessed 10 February 2022].

Paley, V. G., 1981. *Wally's stories: Conversations in the kindergarten*. Cambridge, MA: Harvard University Press.

Paley, V. G., 1990. *The boy who would be a helicopter: The use of storytelling in the classroom*. Cambridge, MA: Harvard University Press.

Pallasmaa, J., 2012. *The eyes of the skin: Architecture and the senses*. 3rd ed. Chichester: John Wiley and Sons.

Pardo, A. with Golbach, J. (eds.) 2018. *Dorothea Lange: Politics of seeing*. London and Paris: Prestel Publishing Ltd. in association with Barbican Art Gallery and Jeu de Paume.

Pascal, C., and Bertram, T., 2021. What do young children have to say? Recognising their voices, wisdom, agency and need for companionship during the COVID pandemic. *European Early Childhood Education Research Journal*, 29 (1), 21–34.

Paterson, G., 2022. Marvellous mealtimes at Bowhouse early learning and childcare setting in Scotland. *In:* L. Arnott and K. Wall, eds. *The theory and practice of voice in early childhood: An international exploration*. London: Routledge, 133–142.

Payne, P. G., and Wattchow, B., 2009. Phenomenological deconstruction, slow pedagogy and the corporeal turn in wild environment/outdoor education. *Canadian Journal of Environmental Education*, 14 (1), 15–32.

Pettersvold, M., 2012. Medvirkning, danning og demokrati i barnehagen: En casestudie av et prosjektarbeid om bærekraftig utvikling. *BARN-Forskning om barn og barndom i Norden*, 30 (2), 23–42.

Pettersvold, M., and Nordtømme, S., 2019. På kryss og tversi i barnas fotografier. Barns fotografiske ytringer. Barnehagefolk, (3), 26–53.

Pinar, W., and Irwin, R., eds. 2005. *Curriculum in a new key: The collected works of Ted Aoki*. Mahwah, NJ: Lawrence Erlbaum.

Povey, H., Boylan, M., and Adams, G., 2021. Regulated time and expansive time in primary school mathematics. Pedagogy, Culture and Society, 29 (1), 119–136.

Powell, S., McMullen, M., Rockel, J., Cooper, M., and Siu, C. T. S., 2019. Pedagogies of care for one-year-olds: A collaborative, cross-national study. Paper presented at the 29th European Early Childhood Education Research Association Conference (EECERA 2019), Thessaloniki.

Rajabali, A., 2022. Whirling with Aoki at the cross of horizontal and vertical intentions: A poet's pondering with/in language and light. *In:* N. Lee, L. Wong, and J. Ursino, eds. *Lingering with the works of Ted Aoki: Historical and contemporary significance for curriculum research and practice*. New York, Routledge, 33–45.

Rinaldi, C., 2005. Documentation and assessment: What is the relationship? *In:* A. Clark, A. T. Kjørholt and P. Moss, eds. *Beyond listening: Children's perspectives on early childhood services*. Bristol: Policy Press, 17–28.

Rinaldi, C., 2006. *In dialogue with Reggio Emilia: Listening, researching and learning*. London: Routledge.

Robert-Holmes, G., 2020. Towards a pluralist and participatory accountability. *In:* C. Cameron and P. Moss, eds. *Transforming early childhood in England: Towards a democratic education*. London: UCL Press, 170–187.

Robert-Holmes, G., and Bradbury, A., 2016. Governance, accountability and the datification of early years education in England. *British Educational Research Journal*, 42 (4), 600–613.

Robert-Holmes, G., and Moss, P., 2021. *Neoliberalism and early childhood education: Markets, imaginaries and governance*. London: Routledge.

Rosa, H., 2019. *Resonance: A sociology of our relationship to the world*. Hoboken, NJ: Wiley.

Rose, G., 2016. *Visual methodologies: An introduction to researching with visual methods*. 4th ed. London: SAGE.

Rose, N., 1999. *Powers of Freedom: Reframing political thought*. Cambridge: Cambridge University Press.

Rose, S., and Whitty, P., 2010. "Where do we find the time to do this?" Struggling against the Tyranny of time. *The Alberta Journal of Educational Research*, 56 (3), 257–273.

Rovelli, C., 2018. *The order of time*. London: Allen Lane.

Schatzki, T. R., 2006. The time of activity. *Continental Philosophy Review*, 39 (2), 155–182. https://doi.org/10.1007/s11007-006-9026-1.

Scottish Government, 2013. *Play strategy for Scotland: Our vision*. Edinburgh: Scottish Government Source: http://www.scotland.gov.uk/Publications/2013/06/5675.

Seeber, B., and Berg, M., 2016. *The slow professor: Challenging the culture of speed in the academy*. Toronto: University of Toronto Press.

Senge, P. M., Scharmer, C. O., Jaworski, J., and Flowers, B. S., 2008. *Presence: Exploring profound change in people, organizations and society*. Boston, MA: Nicholas Brealey Publishing.

Serres, M. with Latour, B., 1990. *Conversations on science, culture and time*. Ann Arbor, MI: University of Michigan Press. Memo- original citing of this quote in Burke and grosvenor cite as Serres and then put Serres with Latour in ref.

Shahjahan, R., 2015. Being lazy' and slowing down: Towards decolonizing time, our body and pedagogy. *Educational Philosophy and Theory*, 47 (5), 488–501.

Sherringham, M., 2006. *Everyday life: Theories and practices from surrealism to the present*. 1st ed. Oxford: Oxford University Press.

Sibieta, L., 2021. The crisis in lost learning calls for a massive national policy response. *Institute of Fiscal Studies Bulletin*, 1 February. Available from: https://ifs.org.uk/publications/15291 [Accessed 10 February 2022].

Swinton, J., 2016. *Becoming friends of time: Disability, timefullness and gentle discipleship*. London: SCM Press.

Tal, C., 2014. Introduction of an emergent curriculum and an inclusive pedagogy in a traditional setting in Israel: A case study. *International Journal of Early Years Education*, 22 (2), 141–155.

Tal, C., Fares, E., Azmi, R., and Waab, W., 2008. Beyond learning and teaching in preschool free-play centers in Dalyat el-Carmel and Isfiya. *Early Childhood Education Journal*, 36, 281–289.

Tal, C., and Segal-Drori, O., 2015. Student teachers' implementation and understanding of repeated picture-book reading in preschools. *Australian Journal of Teacher Education*, 40 (1), 15–35.

Tampio, N., 2021. Kids need to play this summer, not catch up on school. *The Washington Post*, 22 February. Available from: www.washingtonpost.com/outlook/2021/02/22/summer-school-pandemic-kids/ [Accessed 21 January 2022].

Taylor, A., and Giugni, M., 2012. Common worlds: Reconceptualising inclusion in early childhood communities. *Contemporary Issues in Early Childhood*, 13 (2), 108–119.

Tishman, S., 2018. *Slow looking: The art and practice of learning through observation*. New York: Routledge.

Tobin, J., Hsueh, Y., and Karasawa, M., 2009. *Pre-school in three cultures revisited: Japan, China and United States*. Chicago, IL: Chicago University Press.

Tobin, J., Wu, D., and Davidson, D., 1989. *Pre-school in three cultures: Japan, China and United States*. New Haven, CT: Yale University Press.

Tovey, H., 2017. *Bringing the Froebel approach to early years practice*. 2nd ed. London: Routledge.

Triggs, V., Irwin, R., and Leggo, C., 2014. Walking art: Sustaining ourselves as arts educators. *Visual Inquiry*, 3 (1), 21–34.

Twitter, 2006. Available from: https://about.twitter.com [Accessed 10 February 2022].

Uprichard, E., 2008. Children as 'being and becomings': Children, childhood and temporality. *Children & Society*, 22 (4), 303–313. https://doi.org/10.1111/j.1099–0860.2007.00110.x.

Valentine, M., 2006. *The Reggio Emilia approach to early years education*. 2nd ed. Glasgow: Learning and Teaching Scotland.

Vandenbroeck, M., 2020. Measuring the young child: On facts, figures and ideologies in early childhood. *Ethics and Education*, 15 (4), 413–425. https://doi.org/10.1080/17449 642.2020.1824096.

Van Manen, M., 1991. *The tact of teaching: The meaning of pedagogical thoughtfulness*. London, ON: Althouse Press.

Van Manen, M., 2016. *Pedagogical tact: Knowing what to do when you don't know what to do*. London: Routledge.

Vecchi, V., 2010. *Art and creativity in Reggio Emilia: Exploring the role and potential of ateliers in early childhood education*. London: Routledge.

Volante, L., ed., 2018. *The PISA effect on global educational governance*. New York: Routledge.

Waddell, M. (1992). *Owl babies*. 2nd ed. Somerville, MA: Candlewick Press.

Waller, T., 2006. "Don't come too close to my octopus tree": Recording and evaluating young children's perspectives on outdoor learning. *Children Youth and Environments*, 16 (2), 75–104.

Waters, J., and Bateman, A., 2015. Revealing the interactional features of learning and teaching moments in outdoor activity. *European Early Childhood Education Research Journal*, 23 (2), 264–276.

Wellesley-Smith, C., 2015. *Slow stitch: Mindful and contemplative textile art*. London: Batsford.

Werth, L., 2019. Froebel's contribution to early childhood pedagogy. *In:* T. Bruce, P. Elfer, and S. Powell with L. Werth, eds. *The Routledge international handbook of Froebel and early childhood practice*. London: Routledge, 33–45.

Wien, C. A., and Kirby-Smith, S., 1998. Untiming the curriculum: A case study of removing clocks from the program. *Young Children*, 53 (5), 8–13, September.

Young, S. and Ilari, B. (eds.) 2019. *Music in Early Childhood: Multi-Disciplinary Perspectives and Inter-Disciplinary Exchanges*. Heidelberg: Springer Verlag.

INDEX

Page numbers followed by 'n' indicate a note on the corresponding page.

Printed in Dunstable, United Kingdom